VANISHING
COLORADO
Rediscovering a Western Landscape

Joe Verrengia

PHOTOGRAPHY BY
Glenn Asakawa

ILLUSTRATION BY
Eric Baker

PUBLISHED IN COOPERATION WITH THE
Denver Rocky Mountain News

The Court Wayne Press
Boulder, Colorado

Published by
THE COURT WAYNE PRESS
Post Office Box 19726
Boulder, Colorado 80308-2726

Vanishing Colorado was originally published in a
series of articles in the *Denver Rocky Mountain News*.
Publisher Larry Strutton, President Robert W. Burdick,
and Editor John Temple

Design: Ann W. Douden

Edited for the *Denver Rocky Mountain News*:
Chris Cubbison and George Douglas
Photo Editor for the *Denver Rocky Mountain News*:
Janet Reeves

International Standard Book Number 1-57098-260-0

Library of Congress Card Number 98-88246

10 9 8 7 6 5 4 3 2 1

DUSK SETTLES:

Wheeler National
Geological Site, near Creede.

Contents

AGAINST THE MORNING SUN:

Green bristlegrass stands in a prairie field east of Boulder.

MAN OF DESTINY:
Artifacts from the expeditions of John C. Frémont offer rich insight into the man and his mission.

PART ONE

FRÉMONT'S COLORADO

JOHN C. FRÉMONT SWEPT HIS SPYGLASS FROM THE GLITTERING SNOW-FIELDS ATOP PIKES PEAK TO THE IMMENSE PRAIRIE BELOW. THE MISSION 150 YEARS AGO OF THE NATION'S PREMIER EXPLORER WAS TO CHART THE COLORADO WILDERNESS AND LURE COLONISTS FROM CROWDED, FILTHY EASTERN CITIES TO HOMESTEAD THE MEADOWS AND MINE THE MOUNTAINS. FROM HIS FOOTHILLS PERCH, FRÉMONT REPORTED A LANDSCAPE LOADED WITH GAME AND BIRDS, "BLACK MASSES OF TIMBER . . . DEEP, RICH SOIL . . . AND VALLEYS RADIANT IN WILDFLOWERS, BLUE, YELLOW, PINK, WHITE, SCARLET, AND PURPLE, VYING WITH EACH OTHER IN SPLENDOR." HIS SALES PITCH WORKED.

A CENTURY AND A HALF LATER, IT STILL WORKS. WHAT'S HAPPENING IN COLORADO TODAY IS THE CULMINATION OF FRÉMONT'S VISION OF WESTWARD EXPANSION. BUT AT WHAT COST?

Hundreds of plant and animal species in Colorado lurch toward extinction as millions of people seize their habitats for playgrounds. From the eastern plains to the mountain headwaters of the great rivers, development is rapidly carving and taming vast tracts of critical wildlife range.

The irony is that millions of Coloradans . . . are unwittingly destroying the very same dazzling western ecosystem that they moved here to appreciate.

The Pathfinder's Legacy

Much of the development is springing up along the same routes that Frémont, nicknamed the Pathfinder, traced in five remarkable expeditions through Colorado and the West between 1842 and 1853. Frémont not only covered thousands of miles, he was the first to extensively collect and catalog plant and animal specimens in the region. His best-selling journals and maps, promoted with the help of his politically savvy wife, Jessie Benton Frémont, guided thousands of prospectors, farmers, and ranchers across the prairie and over the Rockies in what was to become one of human history's great migrations. The heavily promoted adventures made Frémont an American folk hero and even propelled him to become the infant Republican Party's first presidential nominee in 1856.

If Frémont returned to the Rockies today, he'd find crowds of people rubbing shoulders with nature all year round, just as he did. But he also would find more trees because there are fewer wildfires and more deer and elk because there are fewer predators. He wouldn't find any grizzlies or wolves. The only bison he'd see are penned in zoos and ranch corrals. Mostly, he'd find roads, dams, farms, ski areas, subdivisions, and strip malls.

Homes, businesses, and hobbies represent billions of dollars in investment essential to Colorado's economic future. Many of these ventures meet environmental protection standards that are among the most rigorous in the world. Yet collectively, Colorado's human expansion is chasing delicate orchids, soaring hawks, cunning lynx, and other rare species from landscapes in which they can thrive—or at least subsist. Survivors are squeezed onto islands of forest and meadow that many scientists fear are too small to sustain a wide variety of native species. On these scraps of habitat, biodiversity—the assembly of life that took one billion years to evolve—is slipping into what ecologists call the "red zone" of extinction. "Biodiversity in Colorado is in a state of meltdown," declared Jasper Carlton, director of the Biodiversity Legal Foundation in Boulder, a group that sues federal and state agencies to protect endangered species. "The Colorado that Frémont saw no longer exists."

The irony is that millions of Coloradans—some of the nation's most environmentally concerned citizens—are unwittingly destroying the very same dazzling western ecosystem that they moved here to appreciate. "Where you see the land start filling up with people," observed Colorado State University conservation biologist Rick Knight, "that's where you see species start blinking out."

Nature's Crossroads

Colorado is a crossroads of biodiversity. It holds within its borders a greater variety of plants, birds, bugs, lizards, and mammals than most other places in the world. It's not difficult to figure out why. Pretend, for a moment, that you are Frémont in 1844, standing on Colorado's eastern grasslands and gazing west. Fifty miles away, the snowcapped peaks of the Continental Divide poke through the clouds. The vista contains six distinct ecological zones: shortgrass prairie, canyons and tablelands, alpine tundra, riverbanks and lakeshores, foothills, and forests. The elevation increases so sharply that the plants and animals in each zone change fundamentally to accommodate to the colder climate and shorter growing seasons. It's the ecological equivalent of standing in Florida and seeing all the way to Greenland—a distance of 2,500 miles.

Within these ecosystems, at least 183 plant and animal species in Colorado are considered threatened or imperiled. About 30 are protected under the federal Endangered Species Act. Another 418 species may be threatened or imperiled in Colorado but are more plentiful elsewhere. Although the lists include highly symbolic creatures everybody knows, such as the bald eagle and the bison, most of the entries are obscure species, such as the Skiff milk-vetch—an inconspicuous plant. Those who would save both the obscure species and the famous are champions of biodiversity, a movement that differs from traditional conservation efforts. Protecting biodiversity means protecting all life—from capshell snails in a small forest lake to Uncompahgre fritillary butterflies pollinating tundra wildflowers. Proponents of this theory say no one species has greater value than another; all deserve preservation.

To Save or Not to Save

But for many people—resort boutique owners, welders fusing new water diversion pipelines, or families building dream homes on wooded mountain lots—saving everything is impractical, if not absurd. Of all the millions of species that have lived on Earth, 99 percent have become extinct naturally, they point out. Many of today's imperiled species are obscure and have no obvious value to us, at least economically. And saving them is expensive. Scientists know of perhaps twenty Mexican spotted owls in Colorado, and a search among the forests and canyons for more owls costs federal agencies $100,000 a year. "Most species on the list are simply not worth saving," said Frank Cesario, an economist at the University of Colorado at Denver. "Many were predestined for extinction anyway."

The argument is a battle cry to some biologists. They argue that biodiversity is the key to maintaining life on Earth. Lose the little species, and entire ecosystems falter. But if you ask them how many of these rare species there are, they can't be sure because there hasn't been a systematic biological survey in Colorado since Frémont's day.

The Pathfinder was not asked to do a biological survey. His job, sponsored first by the federal government and later by railroad barons, was to map promising routes for moving people and goods from coast to coast. The Continental Divide, the Great Basin, and the

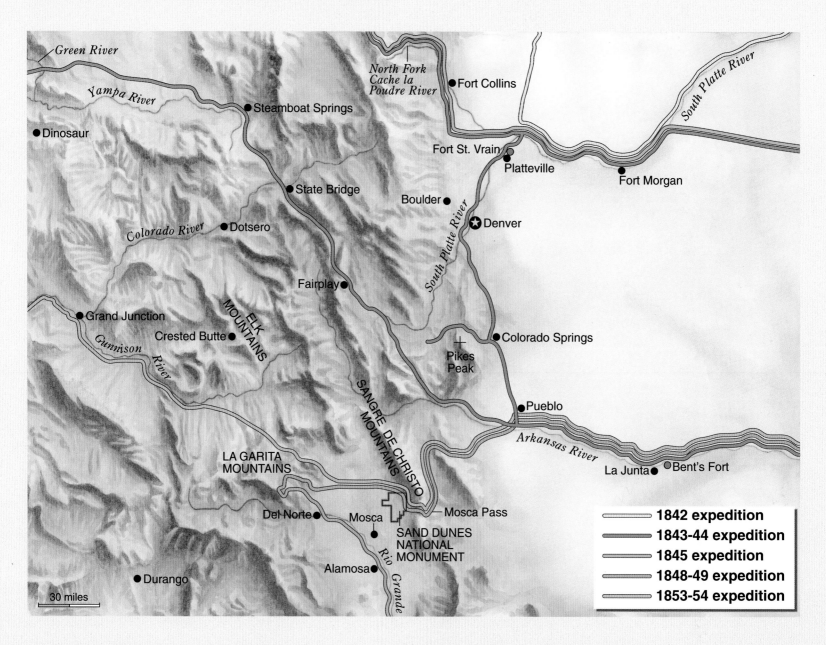

Green River

Yampa River

North Fork
Cache la
Poudre River

● Fort Collins

● Dinosaur

● Steamboat Springs

Fort St. Vrain ●
Platteville

● State Bridge

Boulder ●

South Platte River

South Platte River

Fort Morgan ●

Colorado River

● Dotsero

⭐ Denver

Fairplay ●

● Grand Junction

Gunnison River

Crested Butte ●

ELK MOUNTAINS

Colorado Springs ●

Pikes
Peak

SANGRE DE CHRISTO MOUNTAINS

LA GARITA
MOUNTAINS

Pueblo ●

Arkansas River

La Junta ● ● Bent's Fort

Del Norte ●

Mosca
● Mosca Pass

SAND DUNES
NATIONAL
MONUMENT

Durango ●

Alamosa ●

Río Grande

30 miles

	1842 expedition
	1843-44 expedition
	1845 expedition
	1848-49 expedition
	1853-54 expedition

FRÉMONT LANDMARK:
A shadow cast by Hyman St. Vrain falls on a stone slab marking the location of a supply depot his great grandfather founded. John C. Frémont gathered horses, mules, and other supplies here for his expeditions in 1842 and 1843.

High Sierra, the final obstacles, were his to conquer. But Frémont was a passionate naturalist. Along the way, as he followed river basins and charted headwaters of the major rivers, he collected specimens and described in detail for the first time the biodiversity he encountered in every ecological zone.

No similarly comprehensive biodiversity survey has been done in Colorado since. In 1993, the Department of Interior launched what would become the U.S. Biological Service. This national effort to inventory U.S. species, survey fragile habitats, and consolidate research information into a single database costs as much as $170 million a year. From its inception, questions have persisted about its effectiveness given that researchers have difficulty gaining access to private land to complete their surveys. In addition, a state-level biodiversity survey, the Colorado Natural Heritage Program, has languished—understaffed and poorly financed—for fifteen years. It will contribute data to the U.S. Biological Service as well. Its director, Christopher Pague, said the reorganized program is free from political opposition and is conducting surveys across the state on public and private lands. When clashes do occur, public opinion and the law frequently side with species. For example, West Mineral Avenue in Littleton swerves near South Santa Fe Drive. If it hadn't been designed to do so, road-builders would have steamrolled an American currant bush that is rarely found in Colorado.

But modern-day reality along the Front Range isn't always so benevolent. The Pathfinder's journals are filled with references to bison, elk, and deer from the grasslands to the alpine meadows—and the wolves,

mountain lions, bears, and American Indian hunters tracking them. Development on the Front Range has eliminated most predators. And it has blocked all but two of the historic wildlife migration routes along the Front Range—one near Wyoming and one near New Mexico. Grazing herds are stuck year-round in one or two ecological zones instead of migrating between four or five. "When Frémont was here, the bighorn sheep ranged well out on the plains," asserted University of Colorado mammal biologist David Armstrong. "We've managed to restrict it to its summer range at high elevations year round. It's suffered as a result."

Wild Places Remain

The news isn't all bad. Although Frémont would recognize few places in Colorado today, many of his exploration routes still contain stretches of prime habitat. In some places, such as the Uncompahgre Plateau west of Montrose and wilderness areas near Steamboat Springs, the land remains relatively intact and wild. As the state natural heritage program surveys more of the backcountry, its researchers report finding healthy ecosystems brimming with species. Riverbanks and wetlands, it turns out, are not in universally poor condition. Known collectively as riparian areas, they make up 1 percent of the land in semiarid Colorado but support 65 percent of the species. Never abundant, these soggy places are targets for developers, who covet flat land with picturesque views.

Gwen Kittel, a riparian ecologist, has spent several summers in the 1990s surveying Colorado river basins.

She's found a surprising number of healthy places and not all of them are in protected wilderness areas or private reserves where, in her words, "people have locked the gate and thrown away the key." Among the surprises are some creeks and gulches that were heavily used for grazing, irrigation, and recreation but that now are recovering. For example, along the White River in northwest Colorado, ranchers are noticeably improving their herd management. "It's the first place we've seen native willows outcompete tamarisks and other exotic plants," Kittel said. And between Dotsero and State Bridge, her survey team found pockets of narrow-leaf cottonwood and Rocky Mountain juniper on land owned by the U.S. Bureau of Land Management, an agency that is frequently the target of conservation groups. "The species aren't rare, but the combination . . . is unusual," she said.

But for many scientists—and increasing numbers of environmental activists and outdoor enthusiasts, too—it's not the lists of imperiled species or their exact population that matter so much. The real issue, for them, is how extensively nature has been changed or used in Colorado during the past 150 years under the assumption that nature's resilience was unlimited. Readers of the Pathfinder's journals can hardly turn a page without learning about the luxuriant forage for his horse or the fresh buffalo for his dinner—at least until Frémont reached the dry canyonlands along the Utah border. Expansion progressed under the assumption the bounty would remain unlimited. But it hasn't.

Countless scientific studies have examined every ecological zone in Colorado at every level of detail, from microscopic soil fungi to satellite imaging from 22,000 miles above Earth. But no researcher since Frémont has surveyed Colorado to see what remains. To have avoided, and perhaps actively discouraged, such fundamental work until now strikes many as a betrayal not only of scientific responsibility but of the stewardship of the glorious places the Pathfinder found. "So much of nature was gone before anybody realized it, and we don't know what we had here," lamented University of Colorado biologist Jane Bock. She still reads Frémont's journals as a starting point for her fieldwork on the eastern plains. "If I close my eyes, I can glimpse what it was like when Frémont was here," Bock said. "To not be able to count all of the bison, to have the grasses and flowers growing over your head, to never see a fence or a road—it must have been something."

MOUNTAIN GATEWAY:

John C. Frémont stopped here at Fort St. Vrain on two of his five expeditions through the Rocky Mountains. Examining the historical marker is Hyman St. Vrain, 82, great grandson of Marcellin St. Vrain, who with his brother Ceran established and ran the fort, near modern-day Platteville. "The kindness of Mr. St. Vrain had enabled me to obtain couple of horses and three good mules . . . ," Frémont wrote in 1842.

John C. Frémont is nearly forgotten.

CAMP DISMAL:

Struggling in waist-deep snow in December 1848, Frémont's men frantically cut trees to fuel the fires keeping them alive in the La Garita Mountains northwest of Del Norte. Blizzards, subzero cold, and 20-foot drifts forced Frémont to abandon his attempt at winter passage. Ten men died during the retreat. "We were overtaken by sudden and irretrievable ruin," he wrote.

In Colorado, a county, a mountain pass he never traversed, a prairie knoll near Akron, and a variety of plains cottonwood tree bear his name. That's not much recognition for one of the most controversial and romantic figures in American history—the Pathfinder, whose exploits opened the door to the West and who, at times, eclipsed Abraham Lincoln's public esteem.

As the story of the American West is being reevaluated by historians, so, too, are Frémont's deeds and motives. We're still wrestling with the Pathfinder's brashness and spirit of triumphant conquest over an untamed land. "His ghost haunts us still," observed University of Colorado historian Patricia Limerick. "His cockiness is what we have to reckon with. That's what we're missing now in the post–Cold War era of decentralized power. We're yearning for someone who defies nature, defies the opposition and takes charge. Bill Clinton gets beaten up because he can't be Frémont."

Frémont was so charismatic that men pledged their lives to him. He was a fine topographer and naturalist. His notes and the maps produced by his cartographers are used by scientists today. But a close examination reveals a flawed leader. "The impetuous Frémont often was his own worst enemy," noted biographer Allan Nevins. "He tried to shine in too many fields and by undertaking tasks for which he was ill-equipped, courted not only failure but charges of false pretensions."

Frémont was a remote figure, plagued by insecurities stemming from his illegitimate birth, according to biographer Andrew Rolle. Craving fame and fortune, Frémont made rash decisions that put the lives of his men at risk. He ignored warnings in hostile Indian territory and nearly lost everything running swollen rapids in a raft he couldn't pilot. Early luck pushed him to take greater risks. He crossed the Great Basin and High Sierra in winter. When he tried to repeat his feat in the La Garita Mountains in 1848–1849, ten men died. Rumors of cannibalism on that

Frémont's Personal Path

1813—John C. Frémont born in Savannah, Georgia.

1841—Marries Jessie Benton.

1842—Explores eastern Colorado and Wyoming.

1843–1844—Explores Colorado, Utah, Oregon, Nevada, California.

1845—Explores the West and stays in California. Helps incite Bear Flag rebellion against Mexico. Court-martialed in power struggle with Gen. Stephen Kearney. Later resigns from Army.

1848—Leads winter expedition into Colorado to establish transcontinental railroad route. Ten men die in La Garita Mountains.

1850–1851—U.S. senator from California.

1853—Fifth expedition crosses Colorado in winter.

1856—First Republican presidential nominee. Loses to Buchanan.

1861–1865—Commands Union's western department in Civil War. Frees Missouri slaves; Lincoln transfers him to western Virginia.

1873–1883—Arizona territorial governor.

1890—Dies in New York City.

expedition dogged him for decades.

He was the Republican Party's first presidential nominee in 1856, but he was an aloof campaigner. Secessionists devoured his candidacy and he lost to the lackluster bachelor, James Buchanan. During the Civil War, Lincoln sacked him as army commander in the West after Frémont declared martial law and freed slaves in Missouri. But in doing so, Frémont also widened the political aims of the war beyond the preservation of the Union and probably accelerated the Emancipation Proclamation.

For a time, people loved him. He wrote his best-selling expedition journals with the help of his wife, Jessie, the daughter of the powerful Missouri senator, Thomas Hart Benton. At every turn, Frémont was portrayed as the voice of destiny, the master of this wild paradise. His melodramatic prose about Indians, bison hunts, fertile valleys, and tall peaks spurred shopkeepers and farmers to become pioneers. Little did they know that in many cases the Pathfinder was merely following the same trails that Indians and mountain men had been traveling for centuries. Historian Limerick dubbed Frémont the Path-publicist and the Great American Periscope. "He travels a strip of the plains and the Rockies and he's willing to comment on the character of the entire country. "What he played to was a great pent-up curiosity as to what was out here."

Frémont's later years were marked by failed financial speculations and disgrace. He died at 77 in a New York City boardinghouse in 1890, impoverished and thousands of miles from both his wife and the wilderness that made him famous for a while. He had been seeking the reinstatement of his military pension and a publisher for his memoirs in a last-ditch campaign to rescue his reputation. The best he could manage was obscurity.

Environmental First Aid

MAPPING THE RIVER:
Gwen Kittel and Maureen DeCoursey of the Colorado Natural Heritage Program match an aerial photograph of the East River near Crested Butte with a topographic map to determine the exact location of their survey site.

Ecologists fan out across Colorado every summer to find the state's most imperiled natural places.

CRESTED BUTTE—From alpine wetlands to piño-juniper canyons and short-grass prairie knolls, SWAT teams of scientists catalog every plant and animal species at hundreds of sites. What's rare and endangered is recommended for special protection. What's healthy and lush gets marked as a place to preserve. And what's damaged gets flagged for more investigation and, possibly, restoration.

"We do triage work," said Christopher Pague. "We determine what can be saved, what needs saving, and then go out and find them. We try to hit all of the hot spots." The information collected in this unprecedented survey is being added to a biodiversity database at the heritage program's offices in Fort Collins. The database is far from complete. In the 150 years since John C. Frémont conducted five scientific and mapping expeditions in Colorado, there has been no systematic inventory of the state's biodiversity. Most of the sites being surveyed are on public lands, although private landowners are slowly beginning to cooperate.

On a limited basis, anyone from a butterfly collector to a ski resort developer can check on a location with the natural heritage program to learn what's there—and what's not. The program receives 1,000 inquiries a year, and Pague expects many more as Colorado's growth rate skyrockets and subdivisions sprout in the foothills and mountain valleys. By providing survey data and ecological assessments and by locally accumulating protected pockets of the habitats of rare species, Pague believes his small program can help save those species worldwide. "It's protection in the broadest sense of the word," Pague said. "At the very least, local governments and landowners need to be informed. If a person says he'll do whatever he wants, it may not affect a species globally, but it could have an impact here."

One of Pague's hot spots is a willow-choked valley 9,000 feet above sea level, immediately east of the Mount Crested Butte ski area. One of the largest wetlands in the Gunnison River drainage, it contains a diversity of plant species several times greater than that of the ski area's steep hillsides a few hundred yards away. The East River, a tributary of the Gunnison, meanders down from the Elk Mountains, constantly carving new curves from the valley floor and leaving oxbows behind it. Ecologists say the wetland acts as a giant sponge to filter impurities from river water and naturally regulate flows to reduce flood damage.

Wetlands are becoming increasingly rare in Colorado, and this one is threat-

*Gwen Kittel, ecologist for
the Colorado Natural Her-
itage Program, studies
plant life along a tape-
measured, 50-meter line
on the bank of the East
River near Crested Butte.*

ened on all sides. The
ski area sucks water
from the drainage for
making snow. Cattle
graze on slopes not far
away. Nearby proper-
ties, such as the for-
mer Danni Ranch, are
increasingly being sub-
divided into 40-acre
"ranchettes" for mil-
lionaires. Maintaining
the wetland is "a natur-
al way to have clean
water and wildlife and
it doesn't cost a dime,"
said Gwen Kittel. She
leads the Gunnison
biodiversity survey for
Pague. She also has
surveyed the Yampa,
San Miguel, White,
and Colorado river
basins. "We want to
know what plants are
here but also why they
are here. How sensi-
tive will they be to hik-
ing, draining, and
development? What
species can they sup-
port?" she asked.

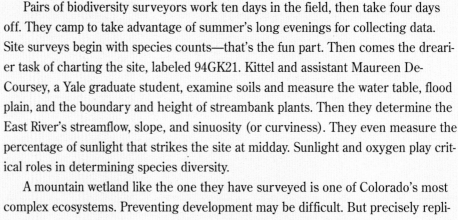

Pairs of biodiversity surveyors work ten days in the field, then take four days off. They camp to take advantage of summer's long evenings for collecting data. Site surveys begin with species counts—that's the fun part. Then comes the drearier task of charting the site, labeled 94GK21. Kittel and assistant Maureen De-Coursey, a Yale graduate student, examine soils and measure the water table, flood plain, and the boundary and height of streambank plants. Then they determine the East River's streamflow, slope, and sinuosity (or curviness). They even measure the percentage of sunlight that strikes the site at midday. Sunlight and oxygen play critical roles in determining species diversity.

A mountain wetland like the one they have surveyed is one of Colorado's most complex ecosystems. Preventing development may be difficult. But precisely replicating the essential functions of bacteria, fungi, and insects in these saturated soils, as well as reassembling the plants, would be impossible if developers claimed the basin and promised to re-create a wetland in another location as compensation. "There have been studies of re-created wetlands that are more than ten years old, and they're still not behaving the same as in nature," Kittel said. "Instead, we should use survey information to tell people to leave the best of what's here. We've still got a chance to protect what we've got."

**CHARTING
THE RIVER:**

*Just as Frémont's explorers
did, botanist Maureen
DeCoursey pulls a string
through the East River to
chart the size of a surveyed
section of land.*

East River Diary

John C. Frémont floundered in snowdrifts and roasted under the desert sun.

TRACKING THE MUD: *Maureen DeCoursey, an undergraduate botanist from Yale working for the Colorado Natural Heritage Program, examines a clump of soil during a survey of the East River near Crested Butte.*

CRESTED BUTTE— But I'll bet he never spent the day up to his armpits in an icy beaver pond. For fun, anyway. And with biting flies orbiting his head.

I joined the Colorado Natural Heritage Program for a day during its summer-long biological assessment of the Gunnison River basin. We were like field medics taking the vital signs of everything that bloomed, swam, buzzed, flew, and roamed along a 150-foot path. From those signs, ecologists would determine whether places like this one are thriving or dying.

The day started with a bumpy ride behind Mount Crested Butte—on the side where it doesn't cost 50 bucks to ride the chairlift toward the summit. I've often hiked, skied, and mountain-biked past these wetlands. But I never imagined I'd be swimming in them—or wanted to, for that matter. My second step from our truck sent me into the East River, a twisting tributary of the Gunnison. So much for a gentle introduction. Then we bushwhacked through shoulder-high shrub willows. The river meanders so much that we alternated between willows and shin-deep mudflats loaded with animal tracks and scat. A close inspection of both the tracks and scat revealed we were nowhere near wilderness. "Let's see," pondered Gwen Kittel. "That track's a dog.

And there's another dog. But those came from birds."

That day it was botanist Maureen DeCoursey's turn to dig the soil pit. The yard-deep test hole enables researchers to examine soil quality. Buried debris—rocks and sticks—would indicate past floods. Her shovel pierced the mudflat's skin. Brackish water oozed around the shovel and over DeCoursey's boots. The muck tried to suck the entrenching tool from her hands. "Oh man, this is so brutal," DeCoursey moaned. "I almost lost my shoes down there." "Hey, this is cake," Kittel retorted. "I'd rather be here than behind some desk."

Tracking Kittel through the willows by glimpses of her hot pink shirt, I forged through the foliage to find the 150-foot line. Every few yards, Kittel placed a metal rectangle painted like a candy cane over the plants growing along the path. The biodiversity was consistent. Below the willows, she found 40 percent sedges and 1 percent wildflowers. The rest was water. The plants strained for sunlight among the dense willows. Kingfishers, dippers, and red-winged blackbirds provided us with an acrobatic air show. "Sedges have edges; rushes are round," she chanted as she counted plants inside the rectangle plot. It's her swamp mantra. However, beyond the obvious distinctions of willows versus grasses versus wildflowers, everything there looked green and wet to me. Sometimes it does to the ecologists, too—but on a more complex level, of course. No fewer than ten shrub varieties could be growing there. "Some willow species really look identical," DeCoursey said. "When they grow next to each other, your head starts spinning."

Suddenly, Kittel found the end of the 150-foot survey line with a splash into a beaver pond. A second later, I followed her in. The mucky bottom turned my hiking boots into concrete shoes. The rain suit that protected me from dew and willow snags inflated with icy, silty water. I looked like a lumpy blueberry. Kittel had already bounded up the bank. She was still murmuring, but she sounded like a priest celebrating Mass as she mumbled Latin species names of the plants she'd spotted. *"Carex utriculata . . . Carex languginso . . . Salix drommondiana . . ."*

If we're lucky, I suggested, a developer would ride to our rescue and drain this fetid swamp for a nice, dry condo village stocked with warm clothes. Kittel just glared. I'm joking. Really. But it's difficult to appreciate the "natural richness" when you're submerged and shivering in it.

Quick—name Colorado's state bird.

If you can't, don't worry—few people can. But what's worse, fewer people now can find one. The lark bunting, the state bird since 1931, may be disappearing—although some individuals can be seen in the Pawnee National Grassland. And Colorado's is not the only state bird dropping in number. The official birds of twenty-one states and the District of Columbia are declining, according to Boulder ornithologist Stan Senner, who investigated them for the National Audubon Society. Official state birds aren't protected from the same threat that other bird species face: loss of habitat. And the lark bunting's plight certainly isn't unique on the Colorado prairie. In truth, many prairie birds could be fluttering toward extinction.

The U.S. Fish and Wildlife Service reports that plains bird species have suffered more widespread declines than any other bird group in this country in the past twenty years. Of 18 species nesting in grasslands, scientists note, only 3 show signs of increasing. By comparison, groups of birds living in other habitats are faring somewhat better. Of 60 species nesting in woods, 37 show increasing population trends; of 41 nesting in wetlands, 26 show increases. "All the grasslands birds are taking it on the chin," said Sam Droege of the U.S. Fish and Wildlife Service in comments to the Audubon group. "The lark bunting shows a big drop on both the Breeding Bird Survey and the annual Christmas Bird Count. It's still super-abundant in some places, but those places are getting harder to find." Scientists blame the losses on the fragmentation of breeding sites by plowing, energy exploration, and suburban development. The slaughter of bison, the suppression of prairie fires, and other widespread natural forces also are implicated. The lark bunting migrates to Mexico for the winter, and widespread habitat losses there also contribute to its decline.

Actually, Colorado's state bird isn't a lark at all but rather a close relative of the finch. Its nicknames include white-winged blackbird, white-winged prairie bird, prairie bobolink, and bobolink. It stands 7 inches tall. Males are black with white wing patches and females are streaked with brown. Their identifying song is a series of rich, warbled trills. They dine on grasshoppers, insects, and weed seeds.

The bunting was not a unanimous choice for state bird. The western meadowlark, mountain bluebird, robin, and long-crested jay were strong contenders. Some birders assume the lark was put forward in a power play by grasslands politicos against the mountain towns. Others say that during the Great Depression, it was cheaper for the state to print photos of a black-and-white bird than a colorful one. A lukewarm plea to lawmakers on behalf of the lark bunting by Roy M. Landgon apparently carried the day in the state capitol. The professor from what was then Colorado A&M University noted that the lark bunting should be the state bird because it is "very conspicuous and can easily be seen from train windows or automobiles."

A RARE SIGHT:
A male lark bunting on the wind.

Sex in the Sand Dunes

SILHOUETTES ON THE SUNSET:

Modern-day adventurers spur their horses up the slope at the Great Sand Dunes National Monument.

MOSCA—It's the sex that drew biologist Michael Weissmann to these stifling, bug-infested pyramids of sand. Sex between insects. "It's a Hollywood tabloid approach to entomology," Weissmann said. "Who is sleeping with whom?"

Colorado's unusual geography means its biodiversity is among the greatest on Earth. And Great Sand Dunes National Monument offers the most outrageous environment in the state. Certainly, nowhere else in Colorado does such a bizarre profusion of insects exhibit such wild behavior with greater specialization.

Let's start with the environment. Everything about the monument is extreme. These dunes are the tallest in North America. Like giant meringue peaks, they rise 700 feet above the floor in a corner of the San Luis Valley northeast of Alamosa. Above them tower several 14,000-foot mountains in the Sangre de Cristo Range. When the air temperature is 80 degrees, the temperature of the surface sand reaches 140 degrees. When winter temperatures plunge below zero, the temperature of the sand below the surface stays warmer. Gales are constantly resculpting the dunes' appearance and even their location on the margins of the monument.

More than a quarter-million tourists slog up these slopes every year, most believing the sand is virtually as sterile as the moon. But the monument actually teems with life: 1 resident mammal (the kangaroo rat), 4 species of grasses, and 580 species of insects.

The insect action begins at sunset when cooler air flushes down the mountainsides to make the sand tolerably warm. Harems, blood sacrifice, and anonymous promiscuous liaisons—it's all rampant in the dunes once the sun goes down. To gather data, Weissmann does the scientific equivalent of peeking through the blinds. "The heat of the day scares everything away. With the heat and the wind blowing the sand around, the insects get pretty beat up. It's at night when they all come out. The dunes at night are fantastic," he said. "Mating is the most vulnerable time for insects, so most of the night is spent in a mating frenzy that takes place under the cover of darkness," he pointed out.

Wasps are the dunes' most common and best-studied predators. The small, black-and-yellow female beewolf paralyzes honeybees and carries them back to her sand burrow. Then she lays her eggs directly on the bees. The larvae hatch and feed on the bees' bodies. The sand wasp uses the bodies of flies in similar ways but provides larvae with additional flies as they grow.

The tan-colored giant sand treader camel cricket isn't exclusive to the sand dunes; it is found in a few other sandy locations in the West. When it emerges from its burrow at night, the cricket is probably the showiest insect on the dunes and a favorite of scientists. Its cumber-some name describes the cricket's appearance and function—2 inches long with enormous, hinged hind legs. Its legs are lined with spines that act as sand baskets to help the cricket dig its phenomenally deep—3 foot—burrows. A hump on its back is thought to contain the complex muscle structure to make those legs dig and kick. The giant sand treader doesn't have wings, so its only means of propulsion is the thrust it musters when it pushes off the sand or burrows down.

The burrows are vital to the cricket's reproduction as well as to individual safety. A male cricket digs a new burrow every day because he roams and the sand shifts. He amasses a harem of females in his burrow every night. He then spends much of his time at the top of the burrow fending off rival suitors.

Weissmann and others study the crickets with techniques such as marking 100 crickets of both sexes with a kind of scarlet letter in order to track them across the dunes as they change harems and lay eggs. But even with so many research subjects, questions persist.

What's "highly unusual," Weissmann said, is that the cricket repeats these behaviors nightly. "There seems to be a new harem all the time, so why spend all of that energy defending something that will change tomorrow?"

PART TWO

THE PRAIRIE

NUNN—COLORADO'S REMAINING SCRAPS OF PRAIRIE ARE LIKE THE OLDEST LIVING WAR VETERANS ON MEMORIAL DAY. EVERY YEAR, FEWER AND FEWER OF THOSE RELIC SOLDIERS SURVIVE THE ICY WINTER. THOSE WHO MAKE IT TO ANOTHER GREEN SPRING AND DON THEIR BAGGY UNIFORMS AND FADED RIBBONS ARE LITTLE MORE THAN GAUNT REMINDERS OF SOMETHING THAT ONCE WAS SPLENDID.

CHANGING GRASSLANDS:

This swatch of prairie near Boulder may look the same from afar as it did in Frémont's time, but native grasses are being overtaken by exotic species brought into the area through tilling or even by the tires of cars.

PRAIRIE LADY:

Enveloped by a panorama of tallgrass prairie, University of Colorado ecologist Jane Bock clutches her copy of John C. Frémont's journals. Bock frequently cites his diaries in her research, which takes her to grasslands such as this one east of Boulder.

Likewise the prairie. On the five occasions John C. Frémont plunged into the uncharted West, he began his journeys by riding hundreds of miles through a dense mat of tough, short grasses spiked with bright yellow sunflowers. The native grasslands of eastern Colorado from Toonerville to Timnath have been drastically changed by a dozen decades of intensive farming, livestock overgrazing, and suburban sprawl. Weeds and hybrid crops have rooted across many thousands of square miles of rolling, semiarid range. Artificially divided into plots by roads and fences, the grasslands are decades removed from their natural state and—in many places—are unhealthy.

One hundred fifty years ago, after a thundershower, the range would erupt in a riot of wildflowers—copper mallow, stemless white evening primrose, prickly poppy, and carpets of birdsfoot violets so broad they appeared as mirage lakes. Bison thundered over the horizon by day. At night, the gray wolf's howl pierced the stillness, and wildfires streaked the black sky orange. Today's prairie looks much the same from afar, a vast ocean of wiry, gray-green grasses beneath an even bigger blue expanse. It's still, in the words of naturalist Audrey DeLella Benedict, "a beautiful, but uncompromising landscape . . . a wilderness of subtle diversity too easily obscured by the beauty of the mountains."

But it's not the same. Patches of the prairie's original mosaic can be found on abandoned railroad beds, unplowed knolls, and cemeteries untended for generations. Like the old war vets, fewer of these relic grasslands survive each year.

What's in a Prairie?

Not knowing the prairie of the past handicaps researchers today. Because everything grows just inches high, the grasslands appear deceptively simple. But without an accurate model, scientists complain they cannot possibly understand the plants, wildlife, and soil organisms well enough to restore the prairie—or, for that matter, decide whether restoration is possible.

"It looks natural enough, but I don't think there's much left out here that is natural," observed Colorado State University range ecologist Bob Woodmansee as he barreled down a dirt road in the Pawnee National

FRÉMONT ON THE PLATTE:

"We found ourselves over-looking a broad and misty valley where, about 10 miles distant and 1,000 feet below us, the South Fork of the Platte was rolling magnificently along, swollen with the waters of melting snow." The river that inspired this 1844 Frémont journal entry today irrigates farmers' crops on the Plains.

Grassland, northeast of Greeley. "Some environmentalists don't want to give up on the idea that we can restore the shortgrass prairie. But there is no physical or biological reason why that would happen. I think we have to forget the idea of going back to something we can only suppose was here before."

After Frémont, surveying the grasslands was haphazard at best. Busting the sod was a way of life, and it rarely occurred to anyone to examine what it was they were digging up. "By the time anybody bothered to look at the real prairie, it was gone," said Jane Bock. With her husband and fellow CU biologist Carl Bock, she frequently refers to Frémont's diaries in her research. "Now we spend an inordinate amount of time speculating as to what used to be here," she said.

The remaining shortgrass prairie is a mosaic of several plants that respond differently to extreme climate conditions from year to year. It contains about 100 shrub, grass, flower, and animal species, but most of them are limited to specific habitats, such as the desert saltgrass in alkaline depressions and the lesser earless lizard in sand hills. In a typical year—14 inches of precipitation and temperatures ranging between 0 and 100 degrees—buffalo and blue grama grasses make up 80 percent of the native plant cover. In wet years, needle-and-thread grass shimmers. In dry years, shorter grasses hang tough. Little bluestem and other bunch-grasses thrive in undisturbed plots where the soil is rich and moist. Where cattle overgraze, prairie dogs burrow, and plows tear the sod for crops, the relentless wind dries and blows off precious topsoil.

Enter cheatgrass, a species from Eurasia that spreads aggressively. "Exotic species are very success-

ful in getting in wherever there is a break in the sod," Jane Bock noted. "Overgrazing in a drought, a hillside slump, bulldozing a subdivision, digging a drainage ditch—they're open invitations for the invasion of outside plants. Eurasian grasses like cheatgrass have learned over thousands of years how to succeed around people's activities, and they carried those traits in their seeds to the eastern plains. When native species try to compete they lose by a mile, she said. "I don't know of any native grasses that are extinct, but there are lots that are very rare now."

Wet and Dry

The secret to the shortgrass prairie is water conservation. Extensive root networks extend 6 feet deep to tap moisture. Tiny threadlike roots at the surface drink up moisture from brief showers. Narrow leaves reduce evaporation. "Frémont described differences on the prairie in wet and dry years, with the grasses coming up to his horse's belly when it was lush," said Carl Bock. "This area is subject to episodic drought in five-year cycles. It's a rigorous natural selection process that is important and underappreciated."

In some ways, the shortgrass prairie is like a tropical rain forest turned on its head. "In the rain forest the competition between species is in the tree canopy," Woodmansee pointed out. "Here, the same kind of competition is happening below ground in the roots." Prairie plants reproduce during drought by sending out creeper roots on the ground and rizomes, or horizontal underground stems, that blast new plants through the surface. In this way, they can survive some livestock grazing and trampling. But overgrazing is their enemy, especially when combined with stream diversion for farm use and a dry summer.

For example, blue grama grass is extensively found. But to regenerate, it requires a warm spring and weeks of cool, rainy weather in early June. That's an unusual weather pattern on the shortgrass prairie, which explains why blue grama may need years to become reestablished after a drought or an extended visit by hungry cattle. "The grasslands are resistant—they can take a hell of a pounding and come back," Woodmansee said. "But they are not resilient. If you break the sod and take it out, its ability to recover is not great."

Assessing Change

Scientists are conducting several new studies on Colorado's grasslands. Of special interest is how shortgrass species interact with other plants on the margins of the foothills ecological zone, as well as how prairie plants cope with a variety of human impacts, including farming. At Pawnee National Grassland, the National Science Foundation sponsors the study and protection of an expansive plot of native shortgrass. It is one of the federal agency's twenty long-term research sites in the United States. The aim is to collect climate, soil, and species data over decades to discover changes and determine if they are caused by humans.

One early warning sign: Air temperatures and soil dryness are increasing at fractional but consistent levels on the Pawnee. It could be early proof of climate

The Comanche and Pawnee National Grasslands represent the only surviving remnants of the once vast shortgrass prairie habitat in Colorado. Common prairie species include:

WESTERN MEADOWLARK

Flute-like song; nests on ground shielded by prairie vegetation

SAGEBRUSH

Thrives in sandy, overgrased soils

PRONGHORN

Thriving and adaptable, despite competition from cattle and farming

BLACK-TAILED PRAIRIE DOG

Competes with range animals for grazing lands

FERRUGINOUS HAWK

Prairie predator; keeps rodent populations in check

BLUE GRAMA GRASS

Dominant plains grass, very drought resistant

WESTERN MEADOWLARK

FERRUGINOUS HAWK

PRONGHORN

BLACK-TAILED PRAIRIE DOG

SAGEBRUSH

BLUE GRAMA GRASS

change, scientists warn. The Bocks are establishing sixty-six test plots in the eastern plains to count species on the shortgrass prairie, from suburban Denver to the state's borders. The studies are so basic that, as was done in similar tests in the Brazilian rain forest, the researchers will try to determine essential facts, such as how big a patch of shortgrass prairie must be to sustain itself. Also, they will try to determine how far away the prairie must be from humans to survive. "We're not trying to prove that the prairie near the suburbs is in any better or worse shape as opposed to the more isolated plots," Jane Bock explained. "There may be no difference at all. But that's the point—we have no prior knowledge of a landscape that has been drastically altered."

Botanists are examining fossil pollen in the prairie soil to determine if the prairie was a different landscape more than 10,000 years ago when the North American glaciers were receding. A different environment would suggest that the shortgrass prairie may not be well suited for today's warmer climate. In this scenario, human destruction would accelerate the ecosystem's in-

Green bristlegrass stands out against the morning sun in a prairie field east of Boulder. Because everything grows just inches high, the grasslands appear deceptively simple.

evitable demise. "The shortgrass prairie more than likely was created under different conditions when there was more precipitation and it was colder," Woodmansee hypothesized.

Here the buffalo come to drink and stand during the heat of the day, adding their own excrements to the already putrescent waters. This compound, warmed for weeks by the blazing sun, makes a drink palatable to one suffering from intense thirst.

—THEODORE TALBOT
TRAINEE ON FRÉMONT'S SECOND EXPEDITION

Frémont's Mapmaker

Charles Preuss wasn't cut out for life on the trail. He was used to gourmet cuisine and soft beds. He tended to be melancholy and grouchy. And he didn't even know how to ride a horse. But he could draw superb maps. That's why John C. Frémont dragged Preuss across the West. The German immigrant's three great works, published by Congress between 1843 and 1848, were the first maps of the territory from Missouri to the Pacific Ocean based on modern principles of cartography. For thirty years, the maps guided the journeys of goldseekers, farmers, and shopkeepers. Preuss's maps were a precursor to the complete topographical mapping of the country by the U.S. Geological Survey beginning in 1879. Fifty-four thousand maps later, in 1991, the project was completed.

Preuss served loyally, but he defied Frémont's order not to keep a diary. Discovered in 1958 and translated from German, the diary has provided scientists with knowledge of the nineteenth-century environment. Historians also use it to examine Frémont's questionable leadership.

June 12, 1842: A lot of rain at night. Slept in a bad tent. Eternal grass and prairie, with occasional groups of trees. Frémont prefers this to every other landscape. To me, it is as if someone would prefer a book with blank pages.

—CHARLES PREUSS

A Prairie Puzzler:

ROCKY MOUNTAIN LOCUST:

Actual size

BUFFALO TALES:

Frémont's journals ominously noted the rapid slaughter of the buffalo in the 1840s.

Why Did the Locusts Die?

Today, buffalo are making a comeback as an increasingly popular food source, raised on ranches such as the Denver Buffalo Company's Sweet Ranch near Kiowa.

A century ago, the Rocky Mountain locust cast a cloud over the grasslands as big as a storm front and just as unpredictable and destructive. History's largest insect swarm, according to the Guinness Book of World Records, was a single cloud of the locust Melanopius spretus that crossed the Wyoming border into Nebraska in 1875. It covered an estimated 120,000 square miles and reached a half-mile into the sky.

Just a generation later the locust vanished. The last of its kind was captured in 1904. It is believed to be the only pest ever driven to extinction. Insect experts lament the loss of the Rocky Mountain locust. As nature's lawnmower, it is regarded as a keystone species that helped define the western grasslands. Rarely has so powerful a natural force disappeared so rapidly and mysteriously. Little wonder, scientists say, that the locust's ecosystem is nearly gone, too. "The Rocky Mountain locust was thought to be the most common insect in North America," said grasshopper expert Carl Bock. "To understand how the plains operated, you have to understand the locust and what happened to it. And we don't know."

In 1990, climatologists drilling ice cores from glaciers in Wyoming's Wind River Range—including the Frémont Glacier—pulled up a series of unprecedented "bugsicles." Upslope winds deposited swarms of insects in annual layers that serve as a biological calendar, much like tree rings. Carbon 14 dating established that the deepest locust layer at about 450 feet was deposited in the early 1700s. "I don't know of any other historical record of specimens three centuries prior to an extinction event," said University of Wyoming entomologist Jeff Lockwood.

The bugsicles are kept frozen. Examining one is a necessarily hasty process dubbed the "rush to the slush." Many specimens are remarkably intact. Some have eggs. Electron microscope studies show they were feeding on sedges and meadow plants when the wind swept them into their icy tomb. Lockwood noted that the frozen bugs match historical references to locusts breeding in fertile river valleys that were being cultivated. Between 1875 and 1904, the prairie's primary grazing animal, the bison, was wiped out; cattle and row crops were introduced. Water was commandeered for irrigation, and

PLAINS REFUGE:
The sun sets behind a tepee frame at the Plains Conservation Center east of Aurora. The center is a sanctuary for plants and wildlife of the native grasslands of eastern Colorado.

the locusts, who laid their eggs in streambeds, were doomed. "It's a classic case of habitat destruction," Lockwood said. "The real irony is the only extinction of a pest was accomplished accidentally. We sure haven't made a dent in insects with modern insecticides."

Farmers aren't grieving. Ten of the bugs per square yard ate as much grass as a cow. During major infestations, pioneers counted hundreds per square yard. The locust appeared like a cyclone after droughts. The horizon blackened and the hot, still summer air hummed with billions of beating wings. The locusts drummed against the dry, cracked ground like a driving rain. They chomped crops down to the roots. They even devoured wooden handles on tools. Trains were forced to stop when rails became slick with locust corpses. Yet, biologists say, these voracious swarms also spread nutrients and removed weak plants. Lockwood observed: "Anything that abundant must have been linked to food chains and dependents."

UNIQUE RANGE:
The irony of Rocky Mountain Arsenal is that because pollution has made it unfit for humans, the land in the shadow of downtown Denver has been left a nearly untouched habitat for prairie animals.

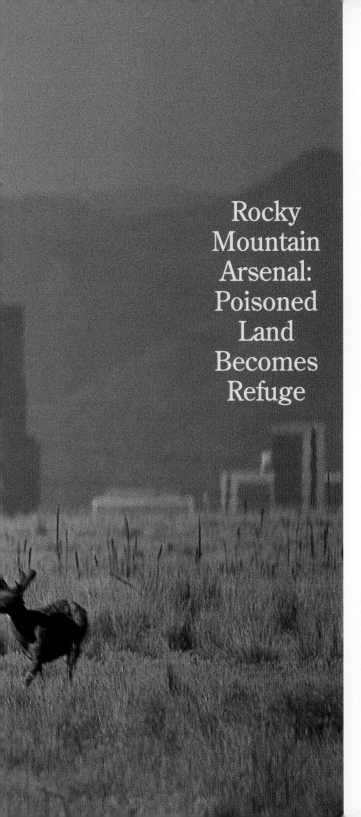

Rocky Mountain Arsenal: Poisoned Land Becomes Refuge

If you squint at the Rocky Mountain Arsenal, the barbed wire and grotesquely festive red checkerboard water tower dissolve before your eyes. What remains looks like the Old West, or even Africa's savannah. Antelope roam the rolling plain. Birds of prey soar overhead. The arsenal's southern range teems with wildlife, which spills into the surrounding neighborhood—rabbits and other ground mammals are not contained by the fences. The arsenal's ponds and creeks support a wider biodiversity than many grasslands sites. Species include snapping turtles, great blue herons, and northern leopard frogs. No comparable area near a major city—except for the game parks in Nairobi, Kenya—bursts with such an astonishing lushness.

Grudgingly, some ecologists credit the arsenal's armed sentries, skull-and-crossbones warnings, even the deadly caches of pollution with saving this landscape from the bulldozers. "The ultimate irony is that without the fences, the remnant prairie here wouldn't exist," said Charles Preston, former zoology curator at the Denver Museum of Natural History. "By restricting human access, biodiversity has been allowed to flourish in ways it couldn't elsewhere along the Front Range."

The arsenal's soil and water still are saturated in some places with residues of chemical weapons, dumped pesticides, and unexploded bombs from its active period (from World War II to the 1980s). Federal auditors contend that a cleanup of the area will cost at least $2.3 billion and perhaps as much as $20 billion. The Army and Shell Chemical Company have already spent $750 million to drain primitive dump sites on the 27 square miles northeast of the former Stapleton International Airport. If the cleanup succeeds, the result will be a wildlife refuge where a wasteland once festered. Preston, who observed that the number of plants and animals at the arsenal is higher than when John C. Frémont explored the area, called this richness a benefit of "managed nature."

In 1996, researchers from the Denver Museum of Natural History concluded a three-year, $450,000 study of how the cleanup will affect the arsenal's biodiversity. It should greatly improve the health of the 400 plants and animals that live on arsenal land. More than half the plants and animals tested since 1989 carried traces of the pesticide dieldrin, which was made at the arsenal and which is believed to cause cancer. Deer mice are especially affected because they dig burrows in dieldrin-tainted soils. Raptors that hunt pesticide-tainted rodents absorb the pesticide themselves. Like DDT, the dieldrin might reduce the birds' reproduction rates. The arsenal is a winter range for hunting birds, which compete vigorously over kills.

Scientists have simulated cleanup operations by cordoning off thirty plots measuring 120 by 120 feet each, which they then plowed 18 inches deep to imitate the removal of contaminated soils. Next they made a computer model to test the cleanup plans. They recommend the cleanup be limited to 150-foot squares connected in a patchwork pattern. Undisturbed plots, they recommend, should be linked together by natural corridors so animals can eat, breed, and travel. In some areas, important food sources could be replanted.

BLENDING IN:

A prairie jackrabbit watches for movement in grasslands at the Rocky Mountain Arsenal just northeast of Denver. Nature's resilience in the face of a huge chemical assault makes the arsenal one of the nation's most remarkable habitats, as well as a major clean-up site.

Creeping Dunes

Geologists fear that a warmer, drier climate is waking dormant sand dunes on the eastern plains. Creeping deserts are a global problem. Poor farming techniques turn 40,600 acres into dust every day around the world. In Colorado, a century of intensive agriculture has eliminated much of the native grassland. Now many farmers are adopting methods to conserve soil and water before sand dunes erupt for the first time in 3,000 years. Some farmers use old tires to hold back the dunes and reduce wind erosion. Others plant native grasses that withstand heat and drought.

Researchers use several methods to measure dune growth. Satellite photos show slight movements. Federal geologists examine sand in a darkroom to determine when sunlight last hit the grains. But not everyone is convinced the sand dunes are stirring. "If the Dust Bowl of the 1930s didn't reactivate the dunes," pointed out University of Colorado geographer William Riebsame, "then I don't know what would."

Prairie Diary

PRAIRIE WEED:
Thunderheads rise over weeds on the eastern plains. Weeds are crowding out many native species on the prairie.

Then I see . . . dark shadows looming on the horizon.

ROGGEN—The miles drone by on the Eastern Plains, with sand hills blending into trampled ranges of cheatgrass and broom snakeweed. The morning sun glares down, turning my truck into a rolling toaster oven. Maybe they should rename it the Chevy Brazier.

Even with the air conditioner blasting, the truck's metal handles and knobs are so hot that when I tune the radio I must protect my fingers with a damp Starbucks napkin. Who says this exploring thing isn't hazardous?

Then I see them—the Rocky Mountains—dark shadows looming on the horizon. I'm nearing Roggen, 80 miles east of the Continental Divide, 50 miles northeast of Denver. This "first glimpse" is the penultimate moment in any trip west. Splashing in the icy Pacific is the only thing better. That's one thing that hasn't changed in 150 years, whether you're wrestling a motor home down the interstate or, like John C. Frémont, riding a mule.

During his first expedition in July 1842, Frémont traced the meandering South Platte River for 150 miles. He resupplied at Fort St. Vrain, near today's Platteville, before veering north. He recorded his first glimpse of the mountains July 9. The weather was hot and hazy, just like today.

Judging by his descriptions, he was near Fort Morgan, about 35 miles east of my present position.

"This morning we caught a faint glimpse of the Rocky Mountains, about 60 miles distant," the Pathfinder wrote. "Though a tolerably bright day, there was a slight mist and we were just able to discern the snowy summit of Longs Peak showing like a small cloud near the horizon. I found it easily distinguishable."

For me, the mountains don't really organize into definable peaks with snowfields and rock faces until Keenesburg, about 20 miles west of Roggen on Interstate 76. This means that since Frémont's arrival, our postcard view of the Rockies has been reduced roughly by half.

Our shrinking visibility rankles ecologists. "I wish we could see as far as Frémont," laments grasslands biologist Jane Bock. "I think it's because of the smoke and the pollution of the city and dust kicked up by plows on the farms. There have been exceptionally clear days when I have seen the mountains from the state line. To see the mountains on the horizon is like a promise."

SCARRING THE FOOTHILLS:

Where Frémont charted wilderness, Coloradans 150 years later leave more indelible marks. An excavation along Colorado 74 and Stage Coach Boulevard in Evergreen makes way for a grocery store a few miles east of the Mount Evans State Wildlife Area.

PART THREE

THE FOOTHILLS

ROXBOROUGH STATE PARK—WELCOME TO THE COLLISION ZONE, WHERE PEOPLE AND NATURE ARE STAGING A DEMOLITION DERBY. THE PEOPLE ARE WINNING THE BATTLE FOR THE FOOTHILLS, BASHING NATURE WITH BULLDOZERS, PETS, AND PETUNIAS.

COLORADO'S FOOTHILLS ARE A NARROW BAND OF WRINKLES RISING 5,500 TO 8,000 FEET ABOVE SEA LEVEL BETWEEN THE GREAT PLAINS AND THE ROCKY MOUNTAINS. LIKE THE THRESHOLD TO A SNOWCAPPED PARADISE, TILTED RED SANDSTONE MARKS THIS 30-MILE-WIDE TRANSITION ZONE. BUT BIOLOGICALLY SPEAKING, IT'S NOT AN ABRUPT BOUNDARY. IT'S A MID-ELEVATION MELTING POT WHERE PLANT AND ANIMAL SPECIES FROM ALL DIRECTIONS MINGLE.

When explorer John C. Frémont traveled the foothills during the 1840s, he reported "lofty escarpments of red rock. We came upon the pines, and the quaking aspen was mixed with the cottonwood," he wrote. "There was excellent grass and many beautiful flowers. We surprised a grizzly bear sauntering along the river, which, raising himself upon his hind legs, took a deliberate survey of us that did not appear very satisfactory, and he scrambled into the river and swam to the opposite side."

Frémont was standing near this glorious state park southwest of Denver, where the South Platte River spills from the mountains. Consider whether that moment would replay itself now as you golf the manicured fescue fairways of Arrowhead Country Club or bike the asphalt road ringing Chatfield Reservoir. You can see the same red rocks. But thousands of settlers followed Frémont's maps to Colorado. Combined with the influx of settlers suburbanizing the foothills today, they have guaranteed there can't be a grizzly within 1,000 miles of this place. "The greatest threat to our native biodiversity is on privately owned land in the foothills," said conservation biologist Rick Knight. "Thousands of people are subdividing what were large, diverse habitats and introducing exotic species to make it look like home," Knight said. "We're homogenizing and simplifying the landscape."

"A View and Some Trees"

In their natural state, Colorado's foothills are a riot of plant life, a magnet for wild animals and suburban settlers. Gambel oak and mountain mahogany dominate the dry gullies and red rock outcroppings. Ponderosa pines spill downhill to moister, cooler northern slopes. On drier, southern exposures, blue grama and needle-and-thread grass creep up from the prairie. A few tropical plants root in warm, protected pockets. They're stunted from exhaustion and thirst after the 1,000-year and 1,000-mile windblown trek that brought their ancestors north from Central America. Arctic plants have made a similarly arduous journey south.

Of the 49 species of mammals in the foothills, 16 originated in the semiarid highlands of the Chihuahua region of northern Mexico, including the Townsend's big-eared bat, the Mexican woodrat, and gray fox. Many songbirds, including warblers and towhees, are neotropical migrants that winter in Mexico's western foothills and canyons. Very few of these species are classified as endangered. But with the habitat under assault, researchers fear more will qualify. "The foothills represent the northeast corner of the Southwest," said

**FRÉMONT'S
FOOTHILL
ROUTES**

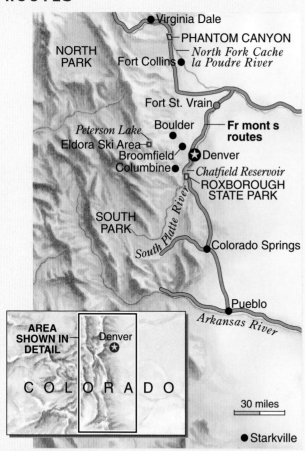

University of Colorado biologist David Armstrong. "They really are an extension of the Mexican ecosystem, and for a good number of its species this area represents the northern limit of their range," he said. "These species are already living on the edge."

Now they must contend with humans and all the stuff we bring with us, including dogs, cats, and greenhouse plants. The numbers are startling. In 1970, Douglas County had 8,407 residents. In 2000, state officials project it will have 132,000, making it by some estimates the fastest-growing county in the nation. Along the Front Range, one-third more people lined up in their cars and sport utility vehicles for emissions tests in 1997 to a record 946,639 vehicles tested, reflecting a crackdown on out-of-state registrations by newcomers to the state. Vehicle registrations increased by about 10 percent in the same year to 4.2 million, reflecting a trend that continued throughout the 1990s. Nearly all the newcomers come from the Sun Belt, with two out of every three of them statewide coming from California, Texas, and Florida. So many of them have never encountered snow that major employers such as Lockheed Martin ask the Colorado State Patrol to give special classes in winter driving.

The growth isn't limited to new suburbs. Jefferson County will have more than doubled in population to nearly 520,000 in 2000, and many of those new residents don't want to live in sprawling suburban tracts. They head for the hills, turning formerly sleepy foothills villages like Evergreen, Conifer, and Morrison into bustling bedroom communities for downtown Denver, the Denver Tech Center, and other employment centers. Since 1960, the number of people living in Jef-

ferson County's affluent foothill neighborhoods has grown from 7,832 to more that 60,000, despite more difficult winter conditions at higher elevations and increased wildlife dangers. In the words of one Evergreen realtor, "They all want to live in the mountains with a view and some trees."

New home sales in Colorado totaled 40,000 in 1997 and the annual growth rate is nearly three times the national average. All those new homes have to go somewhere, and increasingly they are being built on shaky ground plagued by shifting soils, rock slides, and steep grades. In Jefferson County, owners had to abandon at least three luxury homes in Golden that started to slide down the slopes of Green Mountain. The neighborhood was built on what had been designated as a no-build zone for years prior to the 1990s economic boom. Geologists believe more families will encounter similar fates or at least exorbitant engineering and maintenance expenses in the next several years as developers perch more houses above well-documented hazards. "Thousands of homes are affected in the Front Range," said David Noe of the Colorado Geological Survey. All of this development has proven to be a much more effective way to kill wildlife than shooting it.

Islands of Nature

The foothills are 1,200 miles from the ocean, but in biological terms, suburbanization has turned the zone into a chain of islands. For many species, subdivisions are as uncrossable as the roughest ocean channel. So wild animals are confined to smaller habitats. Food dwin-

dles and their chance of escaping catastrophe decreases. This fragmentation is especially hard on big predators such as bear and mountain lion. But it's also difficult for elk and the western spotted skunk. "What we're doing is breaking up an extremely narrow peninsula," Armstrong said. "A carnivore is one step farther removed from the sun than the herbivore. It needs 10 times the area to forage. Anything you do to restrict its range will make it harder to make a living."

Fragmentation is rough on the land, too. Since the 1950s, the Nature Conservancy has spent millions of dollars buying threatened habitats. Now it realizes a small parcel can't resist today's pressures. In Broomfield, the group owns a 12-acre plot. A ranching family willed it as open space twenty years ago. Expensive homes and an office park surround it now. Its plant species must periodically burn to flourish. But fire is too risky and the Conservancy is forced to mismanage the land. "It's a heartbreaking situation," said Alan Carpenter, Colorado land steward for the Conservancy. "Foxes live on the property next door to kids with BB guns."

Species in Danger

The latest of the foothills' rare mammals spotlighted for salvation is the Preebles meadow jumping mouse. Only 200 remain in Colorado, making it even rarer than the more celebrated Black-footed ferret. The mouse's habitat—meadow streambanks—is limited to a handful of sites in Larimer, Boulder, Jefferson, Douglas, Elbert, and El Paso counties as well as southeastern Wyoming. One of those includes the fenced buffer around the closed

WILY INHABITANT:
A chipmunk pauses near the steep cliffs of the Black Canyon of the Gunnison.

Rocky Flats nuclear weapons plant. Most of its range has been consumed by the march of housing developments and business parks along the Front Range.

The 9-inch mouse (mostly tail) could be doomed. But if it can be rescued, precisely how has turned into a bureaucratic battle that illustrates just how cumbersome conservation can become. In 1997, the U.S. Fish and Wildlife Service proposed to list the mouse as an endangered species, which would have put it under the full protection of the federal government even as Congress debates whether to dramatically reduce the scope of the act.

State officials and business interests feared the designation would have given the federal agency control over development of the Front Range, even though fewer than 2 percent is riparian habitat that the mouse favors. And state wildlife biologists wanted to try to save the mouse without the straitjacket of regulations and paperwork that the Endangered Species Act requires. Interior Secretary Bruce Babbit has agreed to keep the mouse off the endangered species list for now and allow state and local governments to oversee conservation efforts. But the federal government still listed the mouse as threatened and reserved the right to supervise the effort.

Babbit said the mouse plan could become a conservation model for other states, but some environmentalists are wary that the plan will allow development to rampage at the expense of wildlife. "We're talking about the rarest unprotected mammal in the United States," said Jasper Carlton of the Biodiversity Legal Foundation. "Reacting to lost causes is the wrong scenario.

States like Colorado should be taking the lead before it gets to this point."

Also very rare is the Rocky Mountain capshell snail. The pebble-sized mollusk lives only in Peterson Lake in Boulder County and a lake in Montana. Twenty years ago, students counted 72 snails per square yard in Peterson Lake. In 1992, only three snails per square yard were found. Nearby Eldora ski area uses lake water for making snow; its owners fund snail-protection studies. Carlton's group has filed for emergency endangered status for the snail.

Wildlife Corridors

Frémont followed wildlife trails through the foothills to South Park and North Park. Bison, elk, deer, sheep, and antelope migrated seasonally between the alpine meadows and foothills ranges. Surviving animals have few gateways to choose from today, even if the numbers of some species have been bloated because of a lack of predators. The result is akin to squeezing elk through a funnel every spring and fall. "How many places can elk move from the plains to the hills?" asked Knight. "There are two places left along the entire Front Range. One is near Wyoming and the other is near New Mexico."

Birds, too, have established migration routes. They cannot breed when faced with the loss of a migration rest stop. "Wipe out or reduce these migratory staging areas," said Colorado songbird expert Mary Taylor Gray, "and the birds, with nowhere to feed and rest after flying hundreds of miles, will die."

Many species mingle in the buffer between the Great Plains and Rocky Mountains, including:

GAMBEL OAK

Often shrubby with deeply lobed leaves

WESTERN RATTLESNAKE

Heat-sensitive pits help it locate a meal

GOLDEN EAGLE

7½-foot wing span; preys mostly on small mammals

MOUNTAIN LION

Powerful enough to kill elk; prefers to stay hidden

MULE DEER

Adapting as people spread across its winter range

WOOD NYMPH

Brown with tinges of yellow

INDIAN PAINTBRUSH

With brilliant red leaves

Close Encounters

Fragmentation baits mountain lion and other predators into deadly encounters with people. Here's how it happens: Foothills suburbanites build homes in the winter ranges of deer and elk. The homeowners fertilize and water flowers, shrubs, and lawns. Deer browse this salad bar. The extra food leads to extra offspring. More deer attract predators. Pets act like prey, and the wild carnivores eat them, too.

Every summer for the past several years, wildlife officers have removed mountain lions from subdivisions in Douglas, Jefferson, and Boulder counties. State wildlife manager Mark Cousins said the inevitable conflicts arise because foothills residents don't take predators seriously. "If they have a lion in their back yard, . . . they call their neighbors to come over and watch."

In Boulder County, county officials have bought 54,000 acres of scenic open space. Voters approved a 0.25 percent sales tax increase to pay for more purchases until 2010. But residents also have opposed a leash law for dogs in sensitive natural areas. "They say, 'My dog doesn't chase small mammals or disturb nesting prairie birds,' " said Jasper Carlton. "All of us must give something up if we're going to protect biodiversity."

FIRE IN THE SKY:
*Smoke from forest fires
enhances a sunset over
the Rocky Mountains.
Unsuppressed wildfires in
Frémont's era created
similarly spectacular scenes.*

Phantom Canyon: *Un-*trammeled and *Un-*changed

Phantom Canyon's real beauty takes a while to reveal itself.

The obvious is incredible—granite cliffs soaring sixty stories high, the

north fork of the Cache la Poudre River glittering like a sterling necklace,

a solitary mule deer nibbling tender green shoots on the riverbank.

But what's truly breathtaking is what isn't here at all. No beer cans,

no cigarette butts, no roads, no noise. No one.

NATURE WALK:
The "very wild and beautiful" scenery that Frémont described in 1843 is virtually un-changed for hikers and birdwatchers in Phantom Canyon 151 years later.

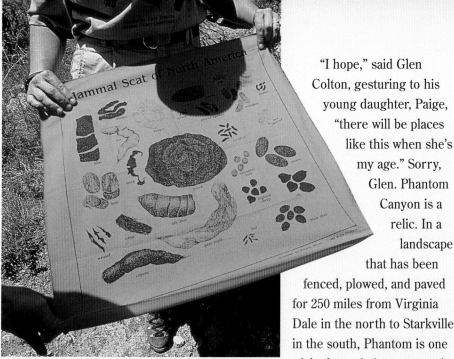

"I hope," said Glen Colton, gesturing to his young daughter, Paige, "there will be places like this when she's my age." Sorry, Glen. Phantom Canyon is a relic. In a landscape that has been fenced, plowed, and paved for 250 miles from Virginia Dale in the north to Starkville in the south, Phantom is one of the last pristine canyons in the Front Range scrubland. John C. Frémont traced this gorge 151 summers ago. It's virtually unchanged.

The Nature Conservancy purchased the canyon rim-to-rim for $2.2 million in 1987 to keep it off-limits to roads, homes, and campgrounds. Visitors need an appointment. Nearby ranchers pledge to maintain a rangeland buffer around it. "It's called Phantom because you have to get right up to the rim to see it," said preserve manager Carol Beidleman. "It's preserved in perpetuity."

The Conservancy and Colorado State University are conducting a year-round inventory of the plant and animal species that thrive in Phantom. The locations and patterns of life in the canyon are being added to a biodiversity map for ecosystem management. Phantom contains a rare parsley plant with yellow flowers, the Larimer aletes, found only in Boulder and Larimer counties. But scarce species aren't what make the canyon special. Phantom is testimony to the umbilical link between isolation and abundance. Rick Knight has cataloged tracks, scat, and other evidence of mountain lion, black bear, deer, bobcat, bighorn sheep, antelope, and an occasional moose. He has rappelled down a canyon wall to measure a centuries-old eagle's nest as big as a bedroom, which is now home to one of the canyon's three pairs of golden eagles.

But songbirds, more than any other form of wildlife, attract visitors to Phantom. The canyon is an important nesting area for dozens of migrants that breed there in the summer, then winter in Mexico and Central America. Songbird populations are suffering catastrophic losses throughout the western hemisphere. Ornithologists say the decline is the most severe conservation crisis since the early 1960s when pesticides all but wiped out the bald eagle and other fish-eating birds. Songbirds run into bad neighbors everywhere. In the tropics, it's settlers who strip the rain forest for hardwoods and pasture. In the United States, it's airports, reservoirs, even golf courses. The bushes and half-dead trees that look like worthless scrub to a developer are luxury condos to birds. That's why visiting this "unimproved" canyon is like sneaking into a songbird recital.

Sweet, sweet, sweet, a little more sweet—that's a yellow warbler.

Chup, chup, zee—that's a rufous-sided towhee.

Chip, pit, zzzd—that's a Lazuli bunting.

In Phantom Canyon, their chorus and their lives are uninterrupted by man.

Homes Darken Doorstep

CELEBRATING NATURE:
Stanlee Colburn exults over
the biological richness of
Roxborough Park.

ROXBOROUGH STATE PARK—
Spying a clump of scarlet trumpet gilia, volunteer ranger Stanlee Colburn gasped and clapped her hands as if this were her first visit to a candy store.

This must be the two thousandth tour in twenty years she's conducted through the majestic tilted sandstone, wet meadows, and impenetrable chaparral of Roxborough State Park. But familiarity hadn't dampened her zeal. One visit will show you why.

The park's 1,620 acres in the Fountain Valley west of Sedalia include one of the state's last surviving transition zones where the plains and mountains mingle. Yucca and prickly pear cactus thrive in the same natural neighborhood as wild roses, buck brush, and aspen, along with the birds and mammals those plant communities attract.

Roxborough was the first parcel in the Colorado state park system designated both a Colorado Natural Area and a National Natural Landmark. The two programs catalog and preserve unique natural features. Roxborough isn't much larger than a metropolitan park. Its serpentine trails total just 12.8 miles. But its biological wealth is greater than that of any one plot on the grasslands to the east or in the woodlands to the west. "There's more life in this little pocket than in any other park I've been in," Colburn said. "The wildflowers at the north end are different from the wildflowers at the south end. Every few feet you see something new."

Development threatens the park and its ecological niche. Already, several thousand people live north of the park and above the red rocks on its west rim. On the rolling, tree-studded meadow immediately east of the park, more than 1,000 homes were planned by U.S. Homes on 595 acres for a subdivision known as Southdowns. The tract has been zoned for development since 1975 as part of the agreement that created the park, but construction has been delayed by bad deals and bankruptcies. Neighbors and conservationists have rallied to prevent Southdowns, and Douglas County and state agencies have committed more than $1 million, including lottery proceeds, in what has become an ongoing effort to purchase the land so it could be included in the park. In 1997, the county and preservationists also purchased nearly 1,000 acres in buffer lands around the park to preserve its character. Now that the Front Range is one of the nation's hottest real estate markets, developers feel double-crossed that some of their most recent customers in the Roxborough area have joined the no-growth opposition. "People move into a community, especially one of pristine beauty, and they want to shut the door behind then," developer Michael Wolff complained.

Roxborough isn't virgin land. American Indians hunted for wildlife amid its cliffs thousands of years ago. More recently, ranchers drove cattle through its meadows. Creek diversions and the elimination of bison and other important species enabled dense thickets of gambel oak and mountain mahogany to fill in Roxborough's canyons. "What explorers saw would have been geologically the same as today, but would have been almost all grasslands in the park," said Aurora Community College biologist Vickee Trammel. "There are many more woody plants now because of the suppression of wildfire and the absence of the buffalo herds."

Red Rocks

The spectacular Front Range monoliths known as Red Rocks are part of the 300-million-year-old Fountain Formation. It is the same formation that runs through Garden of the Gods near Colorado Springs, Perry Park, Roxborough State Park, and Red Rocks Park in Morrison. The red rock layers of sandstone and siltstone, as well as the miraculous angles of their tilting, show the Front Range has been a transition zone for eons. The Fountain Formation was made from debris that washed off the ancestral Rocky Mountains. It was deposited in flat layers and covered by debris.

Two powerful forces made Red Rocks what it is today. First, the uplift of today's Rockies shoved the formation to the surface and tilted it skyward. Then, erosion took over. Wind and water erode sandstone layers quickly, so the remaining layers appear more prominent.

The stone at Red Rocks is red because it contains the iron mineral hematite.

SEARCHING FOR FOOD:

A mule deer in Cache La Poudre River in Phantom Canyon.

Tropical Emigrants

Jorge Mora isn't the only rain forest dweller to immigrate to metro Denver. Some protected south- and east-facing slopes in the foothills contain stunted versions of tropical plants found as far south as Mora's native Costa Rica. As he hiked through Roxborough State Park with Vickee Trammel, together they offered a moving commentary on nearly every plant and creature in their path. "The real special stuff is in the niches of the red rocks," Trammel said, pointing up at the formation's castle-like walls. "It's really shaded, like being in the rain forest."

On poison hemlock: "This is the plant of Socrates fame," Trammel noted. "It hitchhiked into the area in the grain that settlers brought for their cattle. See that red blotch on the stem? We call that the blood of Socrates. You make a tea from the plant and drink it. You feel the paralysis in your toes and it gradually works up your legs and torso. You can touch the plant safely, but I'll wash my hands before lunch."

On harvester ants: "This hill is eight feet across. They eat the fungus off seeds," Mora said. "We have the same ants in Costa Rica. They live in a very different place, but they've developed the same survival strategies."

On mountain mahogany: "It contains a root herbicide so nothing will grow in around it," Trammell said. "It produces these wonderful, hairy seedheads that are self-planting. The seeds screw themselves right into the ground to germinate."

On smooth scouring rush: "This is a very primitive plant," Mora observed. "It reproduces by spores. It's used in Costa Rica as a silver polish and a toothpaste because it contains silica." Trammell added: "Violin makers in this country use it for the final polish on the wood. It's like the finest sandpaper."

Kit Carson

Commemorated by several Colorado place-names—including a town, a county, and a 14,165-foot peak, Kit Carson gained fame guiding three Frémont expeditions through Colorado. Carson spoke several European languages and Indian dialects, but he could not read or write. He already had traveled many of the routes Frémont mapped, including the Front Range, South Park, Muddy Pass, and the Yampa Valley. Carson hunted game, from fat buffalo to stringy sea gulls, to feed the explorers, and he scouted ahead in tribal lands.

A grateful Frémont paid Carson $100 a month and praised him as "gallant . . . self-sacrificing and true." Mentioned less frequently is the harsh vengeance Carson unleashed on several [Indian] tribes. He hunted, and sometimes scalped, native rustlers who stole the expeditions' horses and mules. Under Frémont's orders, Carson burned one [Indian] village in revenge for rustling.

Foothills Diary

Only about a 5% return.

CITY PARK—Every summer, the Colorado Division of Wildlife recruits two dozen volunteers to help remove 1,500 Canada geese from Denver's parks and golf courses. The geese can't fly to freedom because they're molting and haven't grown new "lift" feathers.

Skimming across the park's artificial lakes in kayaks, we herd the birds into shore pens. Head 'em up, move 'em out, Rawhide! Then wildlife officers start handing Branta canadenis over the fence like sandbags—except sandbags don't flap, peck, honk, and splat on you at sunrise.

There's a trick to carrying a wild goose. First, cup one hand over the goose's eyes so it becomes submissive. Then place a finger between its wings and down its spine, and squeeze its wings. I fumbled with my first big gander until the air was filled with fluffy down and the grass around us looked like the floor at a sleeping bag factory. We twirled and flapped in a bad ballroom dance until a burly wildlife ranger whispered: "Grab him like you're carrying a six-pack."

Canada geese aren't native to Denver. They were introduced here and thrived. In 1957, the late wildlife researcher Gurney Crawford created a special brooding flock on College Lake in Fort Collins. The resulting hatch acted like "living decoys" to migrating wild geese that were headed for New Mexico's Rio Grande Valley. Now the resident goose population is 10,000. During the fall migration, about 150,000 Canada geese live along the Front Range.

Park and golf course managers have tried to evict the birds with fireworks, tape-recorded "alarm calls" and even swans, a traditional enemy. But nothing worked. So every summer the Division of Wildlife trucks some flocks to Kansas.

"The goslings won't learn to fly until later this year," said roundup boss Kathi Green. "The older ones get their wings clipped and they won't grow back for a year. Only about 5 percent will return."

SKELETAL REMAINS: *Pines weakened by over-growth and consumed by beetle infestation outnumber healthy trees on a hillside along Interstate 70 near Georgetown. Fires once purged weak and dying specimens, but decades of fire suppression have left Colorado's forests over-populated with trees.*

PART FOUR

THE FORESTS

DEL NORTE—THE LITTLE BLUE SPRUCE LOOKS LIKE THE GRINCH'S CHRIST-MAS TREE—A RUBBERY SEEDLING WITH A COUPLE OF FEATHERY BRANCH-ES. PLUNK AN ANGEL ON ITS WOBBLY CROWN AND THE WHOLE THING WOULD DROOP TO THE GROUND, A SLOW-MOTION STUDY IN DEFEAT. THE TREE IS SIXTY YEARS OLD. NEXT TO IT, A 4-INCH SPRUCE PEEKS FROM THE DECAYING LITTER OF CLEAR-CUT LOGGING THAT OCCURRED A GENERATION AGO ON THIS SLOPE HIGH IN THE RIO GRANDE NATIONAL FOREST. THAT LITTLE SPROUT IS TWENTY YEARS OLD.

Just how long it takes for a Colorado conifer forest to regenerate is startling. Long cold winters, brief cool summers, punishing winds, intense sunlight, and thin dry soil conspire to keep trees in these high forests tiny for decades. At its current rate, this patch—and scores like it on public lands—won't mature until the middle of the twenty-second century.

Need a little context? Consider this—the twenty-second century is the setting for the original Star Trek television series with Captain Kirk and Mr. Spock. Need a historical perspective? A spruce that germinated on these slopes when explorer John Frémont limped through during his disastrous 1848–1849 midwinter expedition wouldn't be ready for logging today. "We thought there would be a 120-year rotation for spruce logging," said Mike Blakeman, an ecologist and educator for the Rio Grande National Forest. "We were dead wrong. We've upped the rotation minimum for logging to 160 years, and it probably will take longer than that."

Very little primeval forest remains in Colorado. Much like the settlers in today's tropical rain forests, nineteenth-century prospectors and ranchers logged vast stretches for mine timbers, railroad ties, and fence posts. Often they torched the forests simply for more elbow room. Forest experts say there are few woodlands in Colorado that do not contain old stumps. "There is some old growth in the San Juans and the Rio Grande, and there is some spruce-fir on the north slope of Boulder Canyon that is too inaccessible to have been logged," said University of Colorado forest biologist Yan Linhart. "There's some old-growth ponderosa pine in the St. Vrain Creek area, and there are small bits of privately owned original forest here and there. But that's about all

I can think of." What remains of Colorado forests, some environmentalists believe, is a "biological desert."

Fire suppression and other policies over the past century have prevented powerful natural forces from revitalizing many woodlands. At the same time, subsidized logging, road-building, and other commercial activities have crisscrossed and, in places, eliminated plant and animal habitats. The results, in many locations where John Frémont explored, are overcrowded, sickly forests infested with parasites. The woodlands are losing their populations of songbirds and other important species. The forest floors are packed with dry timber, potentially as explosive as dynamite.

Logging has been curtailed but has not ended. Lumber companies and forestry officials now mark fewer trees for harvesting and remove them in ways that mimic nature. Foresters today must be able to "read" the ecological history of the area. Where are the elk migration routes? The wetlands that must be protected with a buffer? If bluebells grow on the patch, loggers should know the soil is too moist to regenerate trees. But if Jacob's ladder wildflowers are present, the soil is well drained. If we recognize the forest as a dynamic, natural environment rather than a farm, officials say, logging can be used as a tool to improve wildlife habitat, curtail insect infestations, and salvage trees that have burned or been blown down by strong winds. "Before, we looked at the forest stand-by-stand for its utility," said Rio Grande ecologist Dean Erhard. Judging a parcel on the basis of its biodiversity means asking bigger questions than we've asked in the past," he said.

Chief among those questions is how to keep people from loving forests to death. Coloradans and visitors play hard and frequently in the state's mountain forests. "The next big issue in the national forests will be control of recreational impacts," predicted Jasper Carlton. "Because recreation is everywhere, it could surpass the damage done by loggers, miners, and coal-fired power plants," he said.

Pines in Peril

Old-growth ponderosa pine is the most endangered forest type in the Rocky Mountain West. To qualify as old growth, stands must be at least 200 years old. But inventories show logging and fire suppression have nearly wiped out ponderosas more than 150 years old. Frémont reported healthy, thick pines interspersed with mountain meadows in open, parklike settings. But much of what remains today are bristly stands clogged with as many as 850 spindly trees per acre. Ponderosa pine grows at 6,000 to 8,000 feet elevation on the warm, dry southern slopes of mountains. The slopes are largely snow-free and accessible, making ponderosa easy to cut for mine timbers, lumber, and railroad ties. Of the 194,000 acres of ponderosa pine in the Arapaho-Roosevelt National Forest, just 337 acres—or 0.2 percent—are old-growth. The percentage is similar in Colorado's other national forests. Forest service ecologists statewide say they have trouble locating old-growth stands large enough to serve as study areas. One of the remaining study tracts is in the Manitou Experimental Forest near Colorado Springs. That's where biologists conducted a two-decade-long study on flammulated owls. They used radio transmitters to track the habits

of 200 of these tiny, nocturnal owls, who have an uncertain future because they clearly prefer to hunt moths that live among old trees rather than among secondary growth.

Lost Lynx

Colorado's spruce and fir grow in the highest forested environment in the southern Rockies, beginning at 9,000 feet, where the mean annual temperature is 35 degrees and frost is common in summer. Englemann spruce and subalpine fir drape across the shoulders of Colorado's peaks like a dark green cape. The spruce and fir forest echoes with the rat-a-tat drumming of the three-toed woodpecker and the flute-like song of the hermit thrush.

What's missing are the large, roaming predators—the wolverine and the Canada lynx. After several years of lobbying by environmental groups, including the Biodiversity Legal Foundation, the U.S. Fish and Wildlife Service has proposed listing the secretive lynx on its threatened species list. The Lynx is very rare or has disappeared in seventeen of the twenty states in its historic range, including Colorado. Perhaps 700 remain, mostly in the forests of Montana and Washington. Evidence supporting the continuing existence of the mid-sized predator in Colorado is scant.

In 1998, the Colorado Division of Wildlife did approve a reintroduction plan that would capture 100 lynx and 30 wolverine in Alaska and Canada and transplant them in Colorado over three years. The effort, officials said, would reestablish these predators atop the forest

FOREST

From about 6,000-feet ele-vation to timberline lie Colorado's vast conifer and aspen forests. Some species include:

MEXICAN SPOTTED OWL

A threatened species, per-haps 20 live in Colorado

EBERT'S SQUIRREL AND THE PONDEROSA PINE

Conspicuous ear tassals; dependent on ponderosas, the West's most widespread conifer

COLORADO COLUMBINE

State flower blooms in blue and white

BROAD-TAILED HUMMINGBIRD

Pollinates columbines; male's wings produce shrill whistle

ELK

Large (up to 1,000 pounds) antlered males bugle to attract females

ASPEN

North America's most com-mon tree

food chain in fifteen years. Meanwhile, the U.S. Forest Service approved an expansion of Vail, the nation's busiest ski resort, by another 885 acres—and into lynx habitat where the mountain cat was last seen. What had been a battle of lawsuits and environmental impact statements turned more sinister in October 1998, when a series of fires erupted in the restaurant and lift facili-ties atop the mountain two months before the first group of 40 lynx were to arrive in pockets of remote federal forests from Durango to Vail. A group called the Environmental Liberation Front took credit for the sus-pected arson, which caused $12 million in damage to the resort.

Mainstream environmental groups that were seek-ing an injunction against the Vail expansion con-demned the fires. But they also continued to question the government's reintroduction plan, whose success is predicated on cooperation with a ski expansion that in-cludes clear-cutting trees in the cat's habitat. One irony: Tourism, including skiing, was encouraged to replace traditional industries such as logging and mining, which environmentalists so vigorously opposed a gen-eration ago. Some westerners joke that the most com-mon greeting heard in mountain towns now is, "Can I take your order?"

Environmentalists laugh at the remark, too. But they

AREA SHOWN IN DETAIL

Denver ✪

C O L O R A D O

ROOSEVELT NATIONAL FOREST

ROCKY MOUNTAIN NATIONAL PARK

South Platte River

ARAPAHO NATIONAL FOREST

Rocky Flats

Colorado River

Aspen

Maroon Bells

✪ Denver

TARRYALL MOUNTAINS

Paonia

Badger Flats

Gunnison River

Arkansas River

Colorado Springs

Pueblo

Fremont s routes

LA GARITA WILDERNESS

Creede

RIO GRANDE NATIONAL FOREST

Del Norte

Rio Grande

Cortez

SAN JUAN MOUNTAINS

Alamosa

MESA VERDE NATIONAL PARK

30 miles

FRÉMONT'S FOREST ROUTES

complain that mega-resorts and other examples of "industrial tourism," with large facilities, a huge thirst for water, and strong encouragement from government agencies are not friends to wildlife. What's more, they encourage spin-off development, including the construction of large "trophy" vacation homes that occupy commanding positions on ridgelines but sit empty most of the year. "You can look at the characteristics of the habitat and see that it is good," said Rocky Smith of the Colorado Environmental Coalition. "This expansion would allow for people, and that's not good for the lynx."

A similarly long struggle beckons to protect the wolverine—if it can still be found in Colorado forests.

Biodiversity officials blame its decline on overtrapping and the slicing up of forests with roads and by ski resort development. "The lynx needs old-growth forest in which to den and raise young, as well as young forest in which to hunt its prey, the snowshoe hare," said Carlton. "The wolf is gone, the grizzly is gone," he said. "Why don't people spend any time designing a recovery plan to save species that we still have?"

End of the Aspen?

The highest forests where snow persists until midsummer show less human impact than downslope woodlands, but the scars take longer to heal in such severe growing conditions. Mechanization allowed loggers to cut the steep, remote timber in the 1950s and 1960s. Before that, the only human impact was slow-to-recover burn areas where miners had torched the tree line.

Under natural conditions, successional species (such as aspen) would move in rapidly to fill in the gaps on mountain slopes. They might persist for a century until the evergreen forest could recover. Now, foresters advise, enjoy the aspen's glittering gold autumn foliage while you can. Many forest experts believe Colorado's only upland deciduous forests are on their way out. In fifty Septembers, they predict, the surrounding hillsides could look far more somber.

The quaking aspen aggressively invades disturbed areas where wildfire or avalanches have wiped out the conifers that preceded it. Its quick-spreading stems hold soil on slopes and reduce silt buildup in nearby streams. But many existing aspen stands are elderly, and conifers are reasserting themselves in many places. That's because for several decades public agencies have controlled the natural disturbances that would enable new aspen stands to establish themselves. Logging hasn't mimicked the impact of fire or avalanches, either. Aside from firewood and some paper products, the commercial uses of aspen are limited because the trees are small and the wood deteriorates.

Losing aspen would mean losing animal habitat. Aspen, which grow at elevations ranging from 6,000 to 12,000 feet, provide essential and widespread habitat for more than fifty western mammals. During the winter, elk and deer depend on aspen twigs for browsing. Two dozen migratory songbirds nest in the aspen forest. Woodpeckers, owls, and bluebirds make homes in the cavities that result from fungal diseases that weaken the tree's heartwood. "Some people suggest we're at the upper end of our aspen," said Dean Erhard. "There may come a time when we don't see as many."

It had a beautiful parklike character . . . wooded openly with pine and quaking aspen, contrasting well with the denser pines which swept around on the mountain sides.

—FRÉMONT DESCRIBING SOUTH PARK, JUNE 22, 1844

Quaking Aspen

A grove of quaking aspen reigns as the world's largest organism. Biologists at the University of Colorado estimate the 106-acre stand in the Wasatch Mountains south of Salt Lake City weighs at least 13.2 million pounds and contains 47,000 stems growing from a single root system.

The champion aspen stems appear to be trunks of individual trees. But each of those stems is a genetically identical clone. The Utah stand grew to world championship status by a reproductive process known as suckering. In the West, asexual reproduction can send thousands of stems, or suckers, shooting from a single root system to create a large stand.

Aspen reproduce sexually, too. Male and female flowers appear on separate trees in early spring. A single tree can produce thousands of tiny seeds with long, silky hairs. But few germinate because they are short-lived and must settle on sunny, bare ground. Once a seedling is established, suckering begins.

Modern Mapmaker

Elizabeth Nel rarely wears a backpack when she maps ancient trees. She just fires up her desktop computer. Nel, of the University of Colorado, has developed a program that identifies and analyzes forest images snapped by a satellite orbiting 22,000 miles overhead.

Nel and others have scanned photographs of tracts measuring 900 square yards in the Flat Tops Wilderness Area near Meeker. The computer highlights remaining fragments of towering old-growth timber amid younger trees and rocky formations. The system is far from foolproof. Water vapor in the atmosphere and other environmental factors can obscure old growth's images. But compared to traditional ground surveys, satellite imaging is efficient. "There are so few old-growth stands remaining that we don't have time to waste checking sites with low potential," Nel said. "It's a fast and cheap way to start an old-growth inventory."

The piney region of the mountains to the south was enveloped in smoke, and I was informed it had been on fire for several months. Pikes Peak is said to be visible from this place, about 100 miles to the southward; but the smoky state of the atmosphere prevented my seeing it.

—JOHN C. FRÉMONT AT FORT ST. VRAIN, JULY 10, 1842

The Spotted Owl:

Does It Belong Here?

Fewer than 20 Mexican spotted owls live in Colorado. The question is whether that is natural. Only 2,100 of the threatened owls remain in the United States. Nearly all are in Arizona and New Mexico; about 100 inhabit the Utah canyonlands. Colorado represents the owl's northern range. But researchers can't say exactly how far north it lives. A century ago, Mexican spotted owls were seen in the Colorado foothills, including a place 16 miles northwest of Denver near today's Rocky Flats nuclear weapons plant.

Today the owl's nesting sites are limited to pondersoa pine plateaus and scrub canyons at Mesa Verde National Park and the south-central Rockies west of Pueblo. Researchers have extended their owl survey in forests from Cortez to Fort Collins with no new nesting sites reported. "Historically, the foothills have been the periphery of the owl's range and there's no reason to believe that has changed," said Joan Friedlander of the U.S. Forest Service. Besides human encroachment, harsh winters many have discouraged the owls from staying in the northern foothills. "Its distribution highly depends on being able to prey on woodrats and other rodents," Friedlander said. "That might be difficult under snow conditions."

Conservationists say development has fragmented the owl's habitat, and conserving them as far north as Colorado has biological and scientific value. "Maybe the only ones that will survive global climate change are those that tolerate cold," said Jasper Carlton.

The Mexican spotted owl is a subspecies of the threatened northern spotted owl. The owls look somewhat alike and hoot alike. Both eat small rodents. The northern owl is darker and nests in old-growth forests. Federal protection of the northern owl severely limits the amount of old-growth timber that can be cut. Commercial interests blame the policy for the loss of thousands of logging jobs in the Northwest. But in Colorado, recreation is replacing logging as the forests' primary use as the federal government seeks to reduce below-cost timber sales.

The Mexican spotted owl isn't picky about its home. Surveys show it nests in scrub areas that were recently logged. "The Mexican spotted owl has virtually no impact in Colorado," said Rick Knight. "It's so uncommon and it doesn't require the big timber."

So why worry about a species that was never plentiful? Federal law requires that rare species be studied for recovery. And who knows? The survey might yield surprising results. For example, it wasn't until the late 1980s that Forest Service biologist Richard Reynolds used radio-tracking equipment to learn that the tiny and elusive flammulated owl was the most common raptor in older Front Range forests. It was a case of a mandated study yielding remarkable new insights in what was familiar territory.

Wildfire: Destroyer and Builder

LAID BARE:
A fast-moving wildfire denuded this hillside near Paonia, leaving a wound that will take a generation to heal.

The 1990s will be remembered as the decade of fire—unless the new millennium gets off to an even worse start. The toll has been tragic. In 1994, more than 1,000 wildfires killed 14 firefighters and cost $15.9 million in property losses and $12 million in fire-fighting expenses. Fires sparked within commuting distance of metro Denver in 1996, when a smoldering campfire triggered the Buffalo Creek blaze near Deckers. It roasted 12,000 of the most popular recreation acres in Colorado and burned 9 homes, despite the efforts of 600 firefighters. It will take a century for the forest to recover.

Most of the forests lining Colorado's mountain roads are stands of ponderosa and lodgepole pine on public lands. Born in the nineteenth century, these forests are drowning in their own dead wood on the forest floor, while insects and fungi strangle the trees from above. Eight of ten Coloradans live along these combustible corridors. Virtually every tourist drives along them. It's a catastrophe-in-waiting. Scientists say the reason is obvious and persistent: There's too much dry fuel as a result of aggressive fire-suppression regulations that thwarted one of nature's primal forces. Unlike eastern broadleaf forests, western forests require fire to prosper, but too many land managers and politicians were blinded by a European view that fire only destroys. "We have to teach people about natural regeneration," said Yan Linhart. "It's when we try to manage nature that we screw up."

The ponderosa's cycle is well understood. It grows best in an open stand with bare mineral soils and shafts of full sunlight. Ground fires sparked by lightning naturally maintained those optimum conditions.

**FIRE
DEVASTATION:**

*The blackened remains of a
house and car are grim evidence of a forest fire's legacy
near Paonia. Decades of fire
control ironically helped fuel
disastrous blazes this summer
in western Colorado.*

Fire would sweep through the forest every ten to twenty years, clearing needles, seedlings, and downed branches. Every century or so, a very big fire would burn the larger trees. Audrey DeLella Benedict pointed out that the healthiest trees survived because they had thick, fire-resistant bark that functioned "much like an asbestos suit." Left behind would be super-trees and soil enhanced by ash. Smaller, more frequent fires help conifer forests regenerate. The flames melt the resin in cones, allowing them to open and to scatter seeds on the scorched ground.

But today's monster fires roast the cones. Regeneration comes slower and more randomly. The U.S. Forest Service and other agencies frequently reseed a burned area to reduce soil erosion and weed infestation. In the spring after a fire, grasses and wildflowers grow profusely. Aspen, quick-growing trees that spread on damaged ground, appear soon after. Native pines reach a foot or more in height within a few years. Within a quarter-century, the pines can re-assert their dominance. One Colorado lodgepole stand was found to contain 44,000 trees per acre twenty-two years after a fire.

**FIRE
DEVASTATION:**

*The blackened remains of a
house and car are grim evidence of a forest fire's legacy
near Paonia. Decades of fire
control ironically helped fuel
disastrous blazes this summer
in western Colorado.*

Forest Diary — Don't call me Pathfinder.

BADGER FLATS—It's nearly midnight in the Tarryall Mountains and I've tried—and failed—to plot a course similar to John C. Frémont's, using the stars and a sextant at a spot near where he did the same 150 years ago. On this moonless, cloudless night, the Milky Way drapes overhead like a black gown embroidered with 100 billion sequins. But right now only one thing in the universe is clear to me: If I were navigating for an expedition, we would be hopelessly and dangerously lost in these hilly woods.

Frémont, nicknamed the Pathfinder, accurately made celestial measurements almost every night on his five western trips. He often did it in waist-deep snow and below-zero temperatures. Those readings are the basis for the detailed maps that opened the western half of this continent to settlers.

Frémont's primary tool was a sextant. It's a wedge-shaped optical instrument that measures the angular distance between the horizon and objects in the sky. Nobody actually uses these pie-wheels anymore. It's much easier to aim an electronic gizmo at the sky and let a $12 billion satellite network tell you where you're standing, give or take 50 feet.

But I have to be a purist—with considerable help from University

Frémont used a sextant to chart his course through the West and to create the first maps of the region. This all-night exposure of star tracks (opposite) was made near the La Garita Wilderness northwest of Alamosa. Frémont met disaster here while attempting to cross the mountains in the middle of a harsh winter.

After a few hours, Hibbard gave out. They built him a fire, gathered some wood and left him without . . . turning their heads to look at him. About 2 miles further Scott gave out. They did the same for him as Hibbard.

—FRÉMONT'S MEMOIRS, DESCRIBING HIS PARTY'S FATAL RETREAT FROM THE LA GARITA MOUNTAINS IN JANUARY 1849

of Denver astronomer Robert Stencel and 100 amateur astronomers. So here goes.

Hold the sextant level and, through the eyepiece, aim at the horizon. Adjust the angle of the index mirror until it reflects the image of a star onto a second mirror that shows the horizon. The star lines up along a scale marked in degrees. During the evening, Frémont would make several measurements of a bright star's altitude as it moved overhead. To establish his latitude, he would consult an almanac of known positions of bright stars and calculate the difference from his observed aptitudes.

Longitude is tougher. Observe a bright star's location over several hours and record times and directions. Then recalculate those readings relative to the time in Greenwich, England (designated zero longitude on the globe), and the stars' locations listed in the celestial almanac for those times.

Nobody told me I'd be doing math in the woods.

"I'd be surprised if we get within one arc minute in our calculations," Stencel said. "Frémont reports that he got within one arc second, which is 100 times better. It might've been his best guess."

Stencel and I take turns aiming at Jupiter, then several bright stars. His readings precisely trace the stars' arching paths. Mine read like a Bingo card. At 9:30 p.m., I smugly discover that I am but a single degree off Stencel's measurement of Antarus in the constellation Scorpio. So, Dr. Bob, if we were to use this measurement to meet in the woods, how close would I be? Well, he said, one degree of latitude equals 60 miles. Which means if I planned to meet Stencel in Denver, I'd wind up in Fort Collins.

Like I said, don't call me Pathfinder.

PART FIVE

THE TUNDRA

ROCKY MOUNTAIN NATIONAL PARK—EVERY YEAR, THE MOONSCAPE ALONG THE TUNDRA TRAIL DRAWS THREE TIMES AS MANY FANS AS THE DENVER BRONCOS. IN A LEFTOVER POLAR NOOK, RETREATING GLACIERS, 12,000 YEARS AGO, ABANDONED TINY ALPINE PLANTS TO THEIR EVENTUAL FATE AS A QUIRKY TOURIST ATTRACTION.

Once the tundra was a treeless, windswept barrier that John C. Frémont and other explorers gazed at with awe and fear. Now, most of the visitors to Rocky Mountain National Park conquer the tundra in '90s style—by motoring up steep twisting grades to the roof of the Rockies in their minivans and RVs. The footprints and litter left by three million people a year threaten this meadow of fragile miniature blossoms and buds. More insidious, however, is the air pollution from cars, smokestacks, and farms that rapidly alters the delicate chemistry of life in an environment where the natural pace of change is measured in centuries.

Few visitors realize that despite its current accessibility, the tundra remains a rare and untamed landscape. To find the same mosaic of mosspink, rock jasmine, and 300 other wild plants elsewhere, tourists would have to venture above the Arctic Circle to Canada's remote Northwest Territories. But John Fielder knows. Over a ridge and out of sight, the celebrated nature photographer carefully picks his path across the treeless landscape. For two years, Fielder trekked what he describes as "this incredible glaciated domain" as few have done before—including Frémont, the Pathfinder. Fielder's mission was to photograph every lake and watershed above timberline in the park's 414 square miles—and produce a book of art photography. Published in 1995, the fat volume includes images of 70 lakes and 40 drainages in a wilderness that largely has been off-limits to vehicles, pack animals, and all but the hardiest campers for nearly one hundred years.

The images that emerged from Fielder's boxy, large-format camera were taken in his now familiar style—fluid, whispering, stirring. What's different about this coffee-table book is that the photographs also will serve as a scientific record of the park's environmental health as rangers struggle to manage a fragile ecosystem. Fielder reported that the park's strict rules above timberline have yielded some ironic results. With a few exceptions, such as popular hiking routes to the summit of Longs Peak, overall damage by humans is hardly noticeable. But bulging wildlife populations are lawn-mowing the plant life in the alpine zone, which is very slow to regenerate. "Above timberline, it's in the best shape of any wilderness in the state," Fielder said. "The scrub willow habitat is in the worst shape I've seen. That's because there are too many elk and not enough fires."

Extreme Isolation

Tundra is Russian for "land of no trees." Alpine tundra refers to the ecosystem found in the Rockies from the highest row of trees—typically above 11,200 feet—to the summits exceeding 14,000 feet. Conditions mimic the extremes of the Arctic in many respects. The frost-free season runs for six weeks in midsummer. The mean annual temperature is below 32 degrees. Winds average 25 mph, but gusts regularly exceed 100 mph in winter. Annual precipitation, which is mostly snow, is 40 inches.

The tundra boasts 300 plant species in Colorado. Most of them are gramanoids, or grasses, and cushion plants (those that spread small and low). Ninety percent of the structure of a tundra plant consists of its root system, which stores nutrients and water for the

TUNDRA

At 11,500 feet, forests vanish as plants only inches high take over slopes rising beyond 14,000 feet. Common species include:

BIGHORN SHEEP

In head-butting battles, the ram with the largest horns usually wins

ALPINE FORGET-ME-NOT

Blue blossoms sparkle like gems among the rocks

PTARMIGAN

Plumage molts from winter white to summer brown

YELLOW-BELLIED MARMOT

High-pitched chirp warns the den of danger

BRISTLECONE PINE

Some of these gnarled sentinels are thousands of years old.

BIGHORN SHEEP

YELLOW-BELLIED MARMOT

BRISTLECONE PINE

ALPINE FORGET-ME-NOT

PTARMIGAN

long winter. Descriptions of the tundra could be mistaken for the grasslands, 50 miles east of the national park but about 9,000 feet lower in elevation.

"Both are gramanoid ecosystems with mechanisms to keep woody vegetation out," said University of Colorado plant biologist Tim Seastedt. "On the grasslands, the forces are fire and drought. Wind is the force on the tundra." Tundra plants are varied, but they are not widespread. Each has adapted to very specific growing conditions dictated by soils, wind exposures, snow depth, snowmelt, even rocky ledges. From the distance, all tundra plants look much the same. But get on your hands and knees and you're likely to find six very different plant communities within 100 feet. The brief growing season

means the tundra is vulnerable to damage. Recovery for these slow-growing perennials spans human lifetimes.

It takes centuries to replace soil because there is so little organic material at high altitude. The tundra in the national park still bears scars from the building of Trail Ridge Road in the 1930s. Overgrazing by sheep since the 1800s left timberline meadows battered and butterfly populations depleted statewide. Now these same areas—especially Colorado's 54 peaks topping 14,000 feet— are subject to heavy recreational use. But compared with dammed rivers, plowed prairies, and bulldozed foothills, the tundra, thanks to its isolation, remains relatively pure. According to Seastedt: "The tundra is nearly pristine compared with the other ecosystems."

Elk: Alpine Enemies

Probably no tundra in Colorado has been changed as extensively as in Rocky Mountain National Park. Rangers slowly are restoring the ecosystem to presettlement conditions. But not all the changes are caused by people. Margins of error in growing conditions are so slim in the tundra that small natural variations result in notable differences. Below-average snowfalls during recent El Niño years, combined with warm, sunny springs, prompted tundra wildflowers to bloom a month early—in June rather than July—in some years. Continuing dry conditions caused some wildflowers to fade early, too.

The high timberline meadows are the natural summer ranges for elk and other grazing animals. Hunting wiped out the elk herd a century ago, but the meadows were restocked with 30 animals when the park was opened in 1915. Now 2,000 elk live within the park's borders. During the winter, their ranks swell to at least 2,600. Elk quickly learn that the park is their haven; their natural predators, wolves and grizzlies, are gone and hunters cannot cross park borders. As John Fielder documented, the high elk population has decimated the dense Arctic willows that grow in the moist depressions beneath high elevation ridges. Willows are the tallest plants on the tundra and provide shelter for many bird and small mammal species. The impact of elk on the rest of the ecosystem is unknown. Karl Hess Jr., author of the controversial book *Rocky Times in Rocky Mountain National Park*, warned that the abnormally large elk herds have upset the natural balance of the park, which is moving "toward an ecological Armageddon." Park Service officials dispute Hess's conclusion but agree the elk problem is real.

Danger in the Air

Surveys in the 1980s showed sensitive high-elevation lakes, fish, and soils had escaped acid rain damage. But in the 1990s, new research indicated other forms of acidic air pollution may be harming the fragile tundra. Levels of nitrogen compounds from auto emissions and farms along the Front Range and power plants from Denver to Craig, as well as distant, out-of-state sources, have doubled since 1991 at some research sites. In the short term, the nitrogen can make tundra plants grow more vigorously and stay green longer. Those changes in the plants provide elk and gophers with more food, so the animals stay above timberline longer, which leads to overgrazing. Tests show the tundra is saturated in summer with acidic nitrogen compounds, which seep into lakes and streams and pose a danger to aquatic life. Cores bored from bristlecone pines show nitrogen concentrations 30 times higher than those

FRÉMONT'S TUNDRA ROUTES

AREA SHOWN IN DETAIL

Denver

COLORADO

ROCKY MOUNTAIN NATIONAL PARK

Colorado River

Denver

Alma

South Platte River

Arkansas River

Gunnison River

Redcloud Peak

Uncompahgre Peak

Lake City

Cochetopa pass

Mesa Mountain

38th parallel

LA GARITA WILDERNESS

SAN JUAN MOUNTAINS

Fr mont s routes

Rio Grande

Frémont camps:
Camp Dismal
Camp Hope
Christmas Camp

30 miles

THE HIGH LIFE:
Lichen covering a rock high above timberline contrast colorfully with the clear sky in Rocky Mountain National Park. Like many other plants, lichen adapt in ingenious ways to survive in the high country.

recorded a century ago and about 10 times higher than in the 1980s. "I think we're seeing the effects of atmospheric stressors, and the alpine watersheds are acting as an early warning system," said University of Colorado alpine researcher Mark Williams.

At the Mount Zirkel Wilderness Area near Steamboat Springs, scientists have found acid snow concentrations rivaling acid levels found in dead lakes in the East. The measurements were taken along a knife edge of the Continental Divide near where Frémont passed in 1844. South of Rocky Mountain National Park at Niwot Ridge, researchers have found that the alpine climate is getting colder and wetter. At a similar research station at Pawnee National Grassland near Fort Collins, tests show conditions there getting hotter and drier.

Tundra Diary

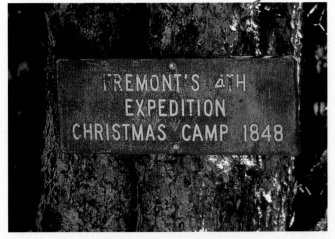

FREMONT'S 4TH
EXPEDITION
CHRISTMAS CAMP 1848

The depth of snow must have been fully 150 feet, as the tops of tall trees were in some places barely peeping through it. [The path] was sunk down in the snow in places 18 feet deep.

—THOMAS SALATHIEL MARTIN,
4TH EXPEDITION SURVIVOR,
IN HIS ACCOUNT, "WITH
FRÉMONT TO CALIFORNIA AND
THE SOUTHWEST"

LA GARITA MOUNTAINS—

It looks like a nice picnic spot,

bursting with forget-me-nots, mountain parsley, and sulfur paintbrush. But the names given to landmarks in this timberline meadow speak to a more ominous time—Difficult Creek, Camp Dismal, and Camp Hope. In these contours 12,000 feet above sea level, during the brutal winter of 1848-1849, John Charles Frémont failed to blaze a railroad route over the Continental Divide along the 38th parallel. Despite crossing the state three previous times, Frémont had little experience above the trees and no regard for alpine weather.

In 1848, Frémont decided, with a dangerous mix of ignorance and ego, that if he could make it over the divide in winter, a train could do it as well. Subzero cold, howling blizzards, and 20-foot snowdrifts blocked his expedition's apparent shortcut to Cochetopa Pass, and stranded the men for three weeks. Even in midsummer, Mesa Mountain and Palmer Mesa carry ledges of snow on their broad shoulders like white epaulets.

But the mile-long meadow is clear, and I need less than twenty minutes to stride across it, including tiptoeing through the marshy headwaters of the Rio Grande. Frémont's men couldn't manage a mile per day. Ten died of exposure and starvation. The survivors bled from their noses and ears, a consequence of the cold and high altitude. Frostbite and hypothermia must have been constant. And there was hunger. First they ate their mules, then their candles, shoes, and rawhide straps. Some men were even said to have eaten the flesh of their dead comrades as storms marooned them in deep drifts.

Frémont's ragged camps have yielded few artifacts. All that remains are bleached tree stumps, whose unusual height—4 to 7 feet—indicates the snow was mighty deep when they were cut for firewood. Federal researchers hope to conduct scientific tests on the stumps, counting growth rings and using Carbon 14 dating, to determine when the trees were axed. They will have to work quickly—several stumps have already toppled. "This is such an extreme climate up here that I don't see why the stumps couldn't have lasted for 150 years," said Vince Spero, archeologist for the Rio Grande National Forest. "Now we're getting into the time period when the stumps are falling. And once they get on the ground, they go quickly."

Even with jeep trails and signs, finding the Frémont camps takes hours. Spero is developing a guide so hikers can negotiate their way by compass. "The existing maps are confusing," he said. "It's hard to know where to go up here, if you manage to get here at all."

TRAVERSING HOOSIER PASS:

Afternoon storm clouds gather over Hoosier Pass and reflect in early summer snowmelt. Frémont climbed nearby Quandry Peak.

Modern Journal Keeper

Jessie Benton Frémont couldn't go. But Gwen Moffat could. In 1988, British writer and mountaineer Moffat embarked on a five-month solo journey to reconstruct the route of Frémont's fourth expedition, which claimed ten lives in the La Garita Mountains in the winter of 1848-1849. Moffat, a former Alps guide in her sixties, was bitten by the same adventure bug that snared Frémont. She benefited from modern equipment and transportation. And she traveled in midsummer, not winter.

Frémont's wife, Jessie, in contrast, stayed home to operate a great myth machine. She rewrote her husband's trail notes into a crusade of western exploration. Frémont emerged in the best sellers as a gallant and tenacious knight. The result was The Storm Seekers, in which Moffat, who also writes Miss Pink mysteries, mingled her personal search in the wilderness with the Pathfinder's. The book has everything," she said. "Flawed heroes, wild country, wilder weather, cannibalism."

Chasing Butterflies

An Uncompaghre fritillary rests on alpine willows. The highly endangered butterfly, not discovered until 1978, is found only above 13,000 feet in the San Juan Mountains.

UNCOMPAHGRE PEAK—Chaos engulfs Amy Seidl even when she's chasing tiny brown butterflies on a remote mountaintop. The wind gusts. Clouds descend. Sleet lashes the steep tundra and rocky slopes just below Colorado's sixth-highest summit. Seidl zips on her survival suit and hunkers down to endure the storm. But just as quickly as the storm rolled in, the sun reasserts itself and Seidl hurries to strip off the same gear before she becomes unbearably hot.

Life above timberline never is predictable for Seidl. When she was a graduate student at Colorado State University, she spent five summers counting the highly endangered Uncompahgre fritillary butterfly on these exposures and a similar tundra site on nearby Redcloud Peak. For the record, Seidl reported having found more than 1,500 of the hardy butterflies on the peaks in the 1990s. That's up from just a couple hundred in the 1980s. She believes the butterfly population is stabilizing—and perhaps even increasing—in its bleak and narrow neighborhood 13,000 feet above sea level. Her data contradict a doomsday declaration by more senior conservation biologists. They suggest the fritillary is going extinct naturally and that scientists and federal agencies would do well to watch but not interfere.

To Seidl, the real scientific question is whether chaos is the normal state of affairs for the fritillary—and, by extension, for all of us. It's a far more philosophical question than asking how many butterflies remain alive. Many biologists find chaos—the inherent unpredictability of events—difficult to measure and disturbing to consider. If chaos is the prevailing rule of the universe, it would mean that life consists of perpetual, purposeless change. Chaos dismisses the idea of a rational, manageable world. According to University of Kansas environmental historian Donald Wooster: "Change is the norm. Disturbance is the norm. The world is nothing but flux and flow." This disquieting notion looms over Seidl's research like Uncompahgre Peak's imposing headwall. But in the meantime, there are butterflies to count.

The fritillary was found in 1978, making it the nation's most recently discovered butterfly. It is thought to be a relic Ice Age species that was trapped after the glaciers melted 12,000 years ago. Now it's confined to mountaintops where the climate mimics the Arctic. In the mid-1990s, the trio of federal agencies that funds fritillary research cut Seidl's combined grant by nearly two-thirds to $6,000 a year. She had maintained nine

Uncompahgre Peak looms in the background as Amy Siedl pauses in her study of the fritillary to seek out a water pipit's nest. The Colorado State University graduate student spent five summers counting the butterflies and thinks the population is stabilizing.

We reached the summit of the dividing ridge, which would thus have an estimated height of 11,200 feet. Immediately below us was a green valley, through which ran a stream. In a short distance rose snowy mountains whose summits formed into peaks of naked rock.

—JOHN C. FRÉMONT,
CROSSING HOOSIER PASS,
JUNE 22, 1844

research plots on the tundra slopes, which she hiked to nearly every day between June and August. Her assistant, Dan Goodyear, used to hike nearby peaks, seeking new butterfly populations.

Here's what Seidl discovered: The fritillary larvae feed only on the green leaves of the inch-high snow willow. A close cousin, the Arctic willow, grows here too, but the larvae avoid it. Female snow willows contain toxic protective chemicals. Seidl would like to do a study that would determine if larvae have a preference for male or female willows or if they have some capability of diluting the toxin.

Adult fritillaries fly fewer than 150 feet in one swoop. Strong winds compel them to seek nectar from moss campion and other low-lying plants. The wind also prevents them from colonizing other peaks easily. Seidl believes the butterflies might billow on the wind to move long distances, which is a dicey way to colonize the high country. "Then the butterfly being dispersed has to be an egg-carrying female that lands on the right slope," she said. The fritillary lives for two years as a larva and ten days as a butterfly. Global warming could extend the short growing season for its host plant and noticeably change the butterfly's cycle. "That's why the fritillary is a good indicator species for climate change," Seidl pointed out.

Colorado's Oldest Tree: 2,442 Years and Still Growing

SENTINELS OF TIME:

Among the world's oldest organisms, bristlecone pines have stood against the wind in Colorado's high country for more than 2,000 years. These are in the Mosquito Mountains south of Hoosier Pass near Fairplay.

Colorado's oldest tree is still growing—but just barely. The gnarly bristlecone pine, its wood sculpted and bleached by the wind, is 2,442 years old—give or take a year. It sprouted from a seed no bigger than a BB on a dry timberline slope near Fairplay during the infancy of the Roman Empire. In the centuries that followed, the bristlecone has recorded dozens of significant natural events in its tree rings, including the Little Ice Age in the 1700s and Colorado's record cold winter of 1912. The history encased in the tree makes the bristlecone scientifically important.

But to many, this sentinel has attained dignity through perseverance. "It's really beautiful," said Craig Brunstein, a researcher with the U.S. Geological Survey. He discovered the oldest tree (which is part of an isolated stand, whose location is being kept a secret) in 1993 as part of a twenty-year bristlecone survey. "My first love has been dendrochronology because tree rings give so much information about what's happened in the past," he said. "Of course, it's in a beautiful setting too." Brunstein visits the tree every few years—despite the difficulty of getting to it. "It gets really hard on my body to visit," Brunstein, 49. "The site is far from the road, and there are some cliffs and talus slopes to climb."

The ancient tree's living tissue consists of a strip of

bark 16 inches wide and a half-dozen branches with green needles. The tree's wide, irregular girth, which measures 30 inches from the pith (or center), signaled its age. Bristlecones generally grow 1 inch or less in radius per century, They limp through the centuries by surviving where no other plant of comparable size can flourish: Bristlecones grow at timberline where summer temperatures are too low to sustain rapid photosynthesis; they need very little water; and the steep, rocky slopes are safe from fires and bugs. The state's second oldest tree, also more that 2,000 years old, stands about 150 feet downhill.

Brunstein has studied frost rings in core samples taken from the oldest tree. They show unusual summer freezes and several cold snaps, including a period around 1815. Volcanic ash in the atmosphere from a series of eruptions cooled the world's climate and triggered summer snows in North America that year.

Bristlecone stands that are reachable by can be found on Windy Ridge near Alma and the Mount Goliath Trail on Mount Evans. Scientists have been marking more vulnerable spruce trees as they creep up the high altitude hillsides and threaten to overtake the millennia-old bristlecones. Given the brief growing season around 12,000 feet, many scientists believe the position of the spruces is a signal that global warming has begun.

Coping in the Tundra

Tundra plants cope with the extreme climate above 12,000 feet in inventive ways.

• The temperature inside a purple-colored flower is several degrees warmer than the outside air because the darker bloom soaks up more of the sun's ultraviolet radiation. But white flowers reflect sunlight, so they remain cool.

• Low-lying, cushion-forming plants, such as alpine phlox and moss campion, attach a tightly woven cluster of shoots to a single, long taproot. The taproot grows deeply into the gravel soil to absorb moisture.

• Old Man of the Mountain has silky hairs on its stem and leaves to conserve moisture. It faces east to capture more sun in the tundra's brief summer.

• The black-headed daisy is covered with a waxy cuticle to reduce moisture loss from blustery winds and abrasion from blowing grit that erodes from the peaks.

• Many alpine plants make anthocyanin, a reddish pigment, immediately after snowmelt and at the end of the growing season. Anthocyanin helps the plants absorb ultraviolet radiation at different wavelengths. It also stores excess sugars produced during cool, bright weather.

ask a more beautiful origin," Frémont wrote of the South Platte River headwaters as his second expedition traversed Hoosier Pass. The window of an old miner's cabin frames a modern-day view of nearby Baldy Mountain.

PART SIX

THE CANYONS

DINOSAUR NATIONAL MONUMENT—THIS IS THE REAL WEST. THE FRONT RANGE IS LOOKING MORE LIKE SOUTHERN CALIFORNIA EVERY MONTH AND MANY MOUNTAIN TOWNS HAVE BECOME ERSATZ SWISS VILLAGES AND FACTORY OUTLET MALLS. BUT THROUGHOUT MUCH OF COLORADO, RUGGED BASINS, CANYONS, AND OPEN RANGE EXTEND OVER THOUSANDS OF SQUARE MILES AND BLEND INTO SURROUNDING STATES.

FRÉMONT'S CANYON ROUTES

Water is scarcer here than in other Colorado ecosystems—as few as 10 inches a year fall in many semidesert stretches. And much of that rain evaporates, so the land seems to bake in a perpetual drought. The plants and animals that hang on in these coarse, salty soils and rocky gullies are grizzled and stubborn. So too are the people trying to eke out a living in such a wide but ignored landscape.

Explorer John C. Frémont opened the West 150 years ago with rhapsodic descriptions of Colorado's lofty peaks and fertile valleys. But in the nine years Frémont spent conducting his western surveys, he spent much of it in these harsh, barren places where water and game were scarce and glory played second fiddle to survival. "Many people don't even think of this place as Colorado," said Patrick Tierney, who has worked for twenty-five summers in the gorges and shrublands of Dinosaur National Monument. "This is what Frémont called the 'ugly, broken country.'"

Yet there are places in this near-desert where tablelands rise several thousand feet from the scrubby floor.

Their margins are grooved by wind and water, but flat, broad summits are dotted with stands of big timber and lakes gouged by glaciers. From base to summit, these tablelands incorporate several layers of plant and animal communities. Scientists for the Colorado Natural Heritage Program recently cataloged the life on the Uncompahgre Plateau as part of surveys of the Dolores and Uncompahgre river basins. Popular with hunters, the plateau remains loaded with a variety of plants and big game, they reported. "We saw a ton of elk. One herd had 30 individuals," said Gwen Kittel. "And I saw a bear and a lot of bear scat. There was no trail and we were just bushwhacking for miles along Monitor Creek. You come across bear scat and you start asking yourself, 'How fresh is it? Is it at least a day old?' "

Survivalist Shrubs

Colorado's canyonlands actually have relatively few canyons. Most of the land is covered with shrubs, survivalist plants that withstand, even thrive, amid the worst that nature can do. Colorado has many types of shrublands. Silvery-blue sagebrush clogs lower elevations of the Western Slope. Greasewood dominates semiarid basins. Dense oak thickets creep up foothills. Just because shrubs are everywhere doesn't mean ecologists can precisely define a shrub. The definition used by natural historian Cornelia Fleischer Mutel may not be scientific, but it does the job: "If you can walk under it, it's a tree. If you have to walk around it, it's a shrub."

Frémont encountered shrublands nearly every-

CANYONS

Hot summers and cold winters in dry shrublands and rugged canyons make life rigorous for many species, including:

QUEEN ALEXANDRA'S SULFUR

Canary yellow butterfly ranges a half mile in its two-week life

AMERICAN KESTREL

Small falcon hovers on fast-beating wings before dropping on its prey

CHEATGRASS

Introduced annual crowds out native species

COYOTE

Despite poisoning, trapping, and shooting, the "song dog" thrives

SAGE GROUSE

Males court on the same grounds used for centuries

QUEEN ALEXANDRA'S SULFUR

AMERICAN KESTREL

CHEATGRASS

SAGE GROUSE

COYOTE

where he went. In eastern Colorado, he encountered a variety of scrub in the dry canyons of the Arkansas River basin, including Royal Gorge. After camping on the Great Sand Dunes in midwinter, he encountered extensive greasewood in the San Luis Valley, where temperatures plunged below zero. Range in the Gunnison River basin is scrubby greasewood. Greasewood and shad scale extend up the Colorado River basin into Eagle County. Sagebrush predominates in northwest Colorado around Dinosaur National Monument and Brown's Park.

Shrubland plants have developed elaborate methods to survive and reproduce. Many conduct chemical warfare in their surrounding environment to deter the growth of competing species. Sagebrush releases terpenes—resinous, naturally occurring oily compounds—to discourage the growth of blue grama and golden aster. The chemical concentration beneath the plant can be sufficiently high to leave the soil bare. Other compounds deter herbivores and other animals by disrupting their digestion and metabolisms and even promoting cancers. Greasewood and prickly pear contain large amounts of oxalic acid, toxic to most animals but not to jackrabbits. Some animals cannot tolerate terpenes, so they carefully graze sagebrush to find plants with low levels of the chemical.

DANCE OF THE SWALLOWS:

Bursting from nests on a canyon wall, swallows soar over the Green River in Brown's Park National Wildlife Refuge. Frémont explored this section of northwest Colorado in 1844.

Shrublands also contain so much salt that a white crust appears on the ground. Greasewood and saltbush absorb high levels of salt and constantly adjust their own chemistry to accommodate it. In winter, the salt can serve as an antifreeze and limit the development of ice crystals in their tissues. Saltbush even has saltwater reservoirs on the hairs of its leaves. These bladders rupture when they are full.

Grazed and Abused

Few people live in the shrublands. Yet, after a century of intensive livestock grazing, it is one of the more damaged ecosystems in the state. Places such as Brown's Park were severely overgrazed by cattle decades ago. When sagebrush is heavily grazed, it regrows vigorously and crowds out more palatable plants. Now much of the land around Dinosaur National Monument and the Green River basin is choked by unusually large and dense sagebrush. Range managers often control it with fire. But wildfire danger is so extreme during the dry summer months that planned burns on public rangeland are limited. Ranges leased to ranchers by the Bureau of Land Management are at the center of the debate over range reform and increasing grazing fees. Endangered species may prove to be the catalyst to reform.

Near Gunnison, the world's one patch of Skiff milkvetch grows in an area threatened by grazing, plowing, and housing development. The Biodiversity Legal Foundation wants the Clinton administration to protect the plant under the Endangered Species Act. A second rare plant, Harrington's beardtongue, is limited to a few small colonies in sagebrush stands in northwest Colorado. Foundation officials said they are seeking its protection, too.

Also fragile are the banks of the region's few streams. To some scientists, range reform hinges on regulating the cows that trample streambanks and degrade water quality. The streams are breeding habitat for several endangered native fish species. Correct water temperature and purity are necessary to keep the protected species alive. "Our ability to prove that grazing causes net damage to riparian habitats and endangered fish in the streams is not quite there yet," said William Riebsame. "But that's where it is headed. Native fish might be a surprising example on the range. People think more about the grouse or other more typical range species. But the fish will be the 'train wreck' that drives range reform." Scientists predict that policies protecting biodiversity, plus deterioration from overgrazing, will reduce the amount of productive range by 20 percent in the next fifty years.

Slow to Rebound

The other impact on shrublands is recreation. Off-road vehicles and ecotourism trips enable thousands of people to rush to these isolated places. Range plants and animal habitat are being trampled, especially in Dinosaur and Black Canyon national monuments, according to researchers. The recovery could take decades, even if some areas are zoned off-limits. The National Park Service, the U.S. Forest Service, and other agencies have limited the numbers of rafters and campers in the most popular areas, such as Brown's Canyon on the Arkansas River. On the Green River flowing into Dinosaur National Park, Tierney and other outfitters are limited to twenty-five customers a day. Tierney's studies by boat, foot, and aerial photos show the human impact on the national monument hasn't increased much since the strict limits were imposed. But the dry landscape still hasn't recovered from soil compaction and campfire rings in sensitive areas that were closed for regeneration in the 1980s. "This is such fragile country," Tierney said. "With just a little use, most of the canyons would show the wear on the trails and bare ground. It adds up to a tremendous impact."

CATHEDRAL SPIRES:
Sculpted over the eons by erosion from wind and water, the Wheeler Geologic Area dazzles.

Ute Ladies' Tresses

COUNTING FLOWERS:
University of Colorado student Ann Hambleton lies on a board to avoid crushing plants as she counts the number of Ute ladies' tresses growing in a pasture east of Boulder. The tiny white Spiranthes diluvialis *orchids are listed as a threatened species.*

TINY BLOSSOMS:
Ute ladies' tresses bloom in late June and July as dime-size white orchids spiraling up a 12-inch stalk.

BOULDER—About 20,000 dime-sized orchids known as Ute ladies' tresses bloom every summer on Colorado and Utah ranges. That seems like a very large population for what is now federally listed as a threatened species. After all, only a few years ago there were just nine California condors and seven Black-footed ferrets in the wild. Botanists say factors other than population size qualify the delicate white orchid for protection.

For one, the orchid doesn't bloom reliably from one year to the next. In June and July, the white flowers form a spiral staircase pattern on a 12- to 14-inch stalk. But not always. A large patch of Ute ladies' tresses near the Table Mesa exit of the Boulder Turnpike has yielded 5,000 individual flowering plants. But fewer than 500 plants may bloom in the same location the next year.

Adding to the uncertainty, the orchids grow on sunny, open range that is becoming commercially valuable—and therefore vulnerable. The flower likes flat ground with a high water table: creekbeds, lakeshores, and floodplains. Those spots always have been at a premium in this semiarid landscape. Besides Boulder, researchers are studying the orchid in the Clear Creek watershed in Jefferson County, at Dinosaur National Monument, in Brown's Park near Maybell, at Deer Creek near Boulder, Utah, and on the Uintah Indian Reservation near Vernal, Utah. These are places where people want to live, ranch, and recreate. "These sites are developing so quickly that without the federal listing the orchid would disappear," said Anna Arft, a University of Colorado biologist. "Its habitat requires active management."

Arft has examined the orchid's genetics and population dynamics. Her discoveries at the Boulder Turnpike location include one big surprise that challenges local ecologists and ranchers alike: Properly managed grazing can help the orchid. During the winter, cows eat Canada thistle and other weeds that would crowd the orchid in the spring. But if cows graze the orchid's flowering stalk in summer, it won't reappear until the following year, she said. Arft has also determined that voles, a type of burrowing field mouse, can decimate an orchid plot. Vole populations have increased because their chief predators, coyotes and owls, are declining as development spreads. But Arft takes a dim view of vole eradication programs. The population of voles fluctuates naturally, she said. And bumblebees, which pollinate orchids, use abandoned vole burrows for their nests. "It's all interconnected," she said.

Sheer and Somber

CLIFF CANVAS:
Molten material forced under great pressure into cracks of the base rock created the lighter streaks on the 2,200-foot Painted Wall in Black Canyon of the Gunnison.

BLACK CANYON OF THE GUNNISON—Geologist Wallace Hansen said it best: "Some are longer, some are deeper, some are narrower, and a few have walls as steep. But no other canyon in North America combines the depth, narrowness, sheerness, and somber countenance of the Black Canyon of the Gunnison."

The Gunnison River carves the Black Canyon for 53 miles across west-central Colorado. The deepest and wildest 12 miles of the gorge are protected as a national monument. Painted Wall soars 2,200 feet above the river. The distance from rim to rim at the Narrows overlook is 1,150 feet but looks a lot narrower. When the sun is in the right position, you can see your long shadow on the opposite rock.

The canyon resisted human impact for millennia. Archeological evidence suggests prehistoric Indians and Utes used the canyon's rim but never ventured below. Frémont's party photographed the canyon on his fifth expedition in 1853, but the pictures were lost. Based on the photographic evidence, the National Park Service credits Ferdinand Hayden's expedition of the late 1860s with being the first whites to document the canyon.

The canyon and its raging river weren't officially charted for another generation. Even then, it took several attempts. Mappers nearly starved on one occasion when the boat containing their provisions was wrecked early in the journey, and it took them three weeks to emerge near Montrose. Those forays enabled workers to blast and drill an irrigation diversion tunnel in one of the great, but most dangerous, engineering projects of the new century. President William Howard Taft traveled from Washington to push a button and open the tunnel, forever changing the Gunnison's wild ways.

*Arrived about evening at a steep
and rocky ravine, by which we descended to
Brown's Hole. . . . Here the river enters
between lofty precipices of red rock . . . the rocks
on either side rising in nearly vertical
precipices perhaps 1,500 feet in height. . . .
The country below is said to assume a very
rugged character.*

—JOHN C. FRÉMONT, APPROACHING THE GATES OF LODORE AND
DINOSAUR NATIONAL MONUMENT ON THE GREEN RIVER, JUNE 7, 1844

FEED ME:

*A baby bird waits for its
mother to return with a
meal atop Uncompahgre
Peak.*

Frémont's Photographer

John C. Frémont brought the first photographer to the West on his fifth expedition. Sadly, Solomon Nuñes Carvelho's original negative plates were destroyed in a Washington D.C., warehouse fire years later. Carvelho lost what could have been an enormous legacy—scores of images of the West a generation prior to the comprehensive mapping and photographic mission by the U.S. Geological Survey. A century and a half later, we still feel the loss of an invaluable artistic and ecological resource.

Carvalho used a delicate apparatus to produce a copper-plate image known as a daguerreotype. Often waist-deep in snow, he would treat a thin sheet of silver-plated copper with fumes from heated crystals of iodine. The sheet was placed inside a large, boxy camera and exposed through the camera lens for several minutes. Then the sheet was developed by vapors of heated mercury.

*We entered upon an ugly, barren and broken country, corresponding
very well to what we had traveled a few degrees north on the same
side of the [Green River]. The Vermillion Creek afforded us brackish
water and indifferent grass for the night. A few scattered cedar trees
were the only improvement the following day; where we halted at
noon we had not even the shelter of these from the hot rays of the sun.*

—FRÉMONT, IN HIS DIARY,
CROSSING NORTHWEST COLORADO, JUNE 10, 1844

Killer Llamas

Colorado coyotes: Beware! Some sheep ranchers are trying a novel way to protect their flocks—terminator llamas. Coyotes and llamas both evolved on the open range of North America three million years ago. Llamas, however, migrated to South America to escape the spreading glaciers 12,000 years ago. In the late 1800s, breeders reintroduced llamas to the United States.

Coyotes, meanwhile, have become arguably the West's most successful large predator through cunning and an aversion to confrontation. They persist—thrive, even—in the shadow of humans despite an expensive federal eradication program. Coyotes have a lust for lamb. Sheep ranchers claim they lose more than $100 million a year to predators nationwide, and 80 percent of that loss is blamed on coyotes and dogs. Livestock growers and the federal Animal Damage Control agency have been waging a determined war against coyotes. In the 1990s the agency shot, trapped, or poisoned as many as 96,000 coyotes annually. The ADC's annual budget is $30 million, 70 percent of which is spent in western states. Supporters contend eradication efforts are necessary because coyotes have learned to outsmart a dozen breeds of guard dogs. Turkish herding dogs are the ranchers' latest breed of choice, but even this large, tough buff-colored canine won't stop its wild canid cousin for long.

Seeking ecologically sound alternatives, growing numbers of ranchers are turning to llama breeders for help. "I'd be looking to discourage the coyote as opposed to eliminating it," said llama breeder Stan Ebel of Masonville, near Fort Collins. "A coyote won't be denied. It has the mechanics to adapt to whatever you throw at it. So I'd be looking to coexist, and the guard llama is the best solution I've seen."

Llamas and sheep are a match made in nature. They bond quickly, graze the same scrubby range, and need the same vaccines. Llamas are brighter than sheep, but they are social animals and tolerate the sheep's dumbbell mannerisms. Sheep, in turn, will follow the llama to shelter when a storm kicks up or danger appears. "Llamas are part of the herd," explains Judy Sealy of the Rocky Mountain Llama and Alpaca Association and owner of Grand Valley Llamas in Grand Junction.

I'd be looking to discourage the coyote as opposed to eliminating it

But one whiff of any member of the dog family— be it coyote, wolf, or Rover—and the stoic llama turns ugly. According to an Iowa State University study, a llama needs very little training to protect sheep from predators. Typically, it will use its imposing height and size to shield the sheep and intimidate the predator. But an adult male llama will also use its 425-pound heft and kickboxer moves to defend from coyotes whatever it considers its harem and territory—including a herd of sheep. Hasta la vista, Canis lantrans. "The llama will issue a shrill whinny as a distress call, and chances are the sound will divert a coyote," Sealy said. The llama also has a pointed toe, and it will propel itself off the ground and come down on the coyote to destroy it."

Canyon Diary

OK,
so we're lost again.

DAVID AND GOLIATH:
A golden eagle flees the pestering of a blackbird that ganged up with others to drive the much-larger raptor off its roadkill meal in the White River basin near Rangely.

SCULLION GULCH—The truck is hot, I caught a case of the afternoon sleepies and we wound up nodding our way to Rangely instead of Maybell. A bemused cashier at the Rangely Kum-n-Go convenience store whispered a secret shortcut to U.S. 40. So now we're bouncing over federally owned sagebrush and a mining concession in the White River Basin. She promised it will save us an hour. Still, we won't reach Brown's Hole until 9 P.M. and we'll have to pitch camp on an island in the Green River well after dark. Disaster? Let's call it an opportunity.

As every honest scientist should admit, many great discoveries come not from genius but from dumb luck and blind turns. Out of the corner of my bleary eye I spy a huge dark bird standing on a bluff. It's tearing at something dead and red. Photographer Glenn Asakawa and artist Eric Baker see it, too. A turkey vulture, we agree.

Hurtling down the road, it slowly dawns on me that vultures . . . don't . . . have . . . gold . . . heads. My tongue is thick from car-napping and eating Doritos. I try to yell "GOLDEN EAGLE!", but it comes out "GOLUMP ARGYLE!"

Somehow, Glenn translates my babbling and whips the truck around. Soon we're standing nose-to-beak with an adult male golden eagle. He's picking at the strips of what was a calf until a week or two ago. Handsome and huge, he regally struts around the roadkill. But what happens next vaults this encounter from a photo opportunity to a biodiversity lesson for the ages. As the eagle rips at his dinner, a formation of tiny blackbirds swoops down to harass him. Fearlessly, they buzz his head and even inflict a peck or two. Combined, the blackbirds weigh far less than one of the eagle's tremendous wings. He's the lord of these western skies, yet within a minute he is retreating.

Circling, he keeps a hungry eye trained on his meal. Three times he works his way back down to the carcass, only to be pestered away. After 20 minutes, the eagle flees down the valley. The pesky blackbirds dive-bomb the carcass even before the eagle is out of sight. We had witnessed a stunning upset victory, like flyweights combining in the ring to beat up George Foreman.

By taking a turn, we had made two important discoveries. Sometimes nature rewards guile and cooperation over brawn and power. And sometimes getting lost is the best way to go.

81

PART SEVEN

RIVERS AND WETLANDS

ORCHARD—PSSST. WANNA BUY A PIECE OF WESTERN HISTORY? IT'S NOT A FADING PIONEER JOURNAL OR A BUCKSKIN SHIRT. IT'S A WETLAND. AND NOT JUST ANY WETLAND, BUT CENTENNIAL WILDLIFE PRESERVE, 50 MILES NORTHEAST OF DENVER IN THE SOUTH PLATTE RIVER BASIN. ITS 715 ACRES INCLUDE A 25-ACRE LAKE AND 50 SMALL PONDS OVERLOOKING JACKSON LAKE STATE PARK AND THE SNOWCAPPED FRONT RANGE.

RIVERS AND WETLANDS

These areas make up 1% of Colorado, but dams and development have all but eliminated habitat for many species, including:

BELTED KINGFISHER
Blue-gray bird swoops over the water in its quest for fish

BLUE HERON
Long-legged aquatic hunter prefers to nest in old cotton-woods

MONKSHOOD
Purple-blue blossoms resemble hoods

RIVER OTTER
A playful animal with hair so dense that water can't penetrate to the skin

GREENBACK CUTTHROAT TROUT
Unique Colorado native has been named the state fish

CATTAIL
Roots are edible raw or roasted

BELTED KINGFISHER

BLUE HERON

MONKSHOOD

GREENBACK CUTTHROAT TROUT

RIVER OTTER

CATTAIL

It teems with deer, coyotes, cougars, raccoons, herons, pelicans, and 13 species of ducks. Biologists have spotted half of Colorado's 600 species of vertebrate animals nearby, making the preserve a biodiversity treasury. It's one of the last places in Colorado that explorer John C. Frémont might still recognize 150 years after he followed the Platte, Arkansas, Colorado, and other rivers as natural highways into the high country. That was when the Platte meandered aimlessly across the eastern plains like a bored child on a hazy summer afternoon. "In Frémont's day, you would have seen a wide, shallow river with limited vegetation along its banks," said Dan Luecke, senior scientist with the Environmental Defense Fund in Boulder. "In Colorado, nothing like that exists now over a large area."

Wetlands are vanishing in Colorado, and that means biodiversity loses, too. With all its natural riches, Centennial Wildlife Preserve could become part of a 15,000-acre national wildlife refuge. Or, its owner, John Andrick, could sell it to you under two conditions: First, pay him several million dollars—exactly how much he won't reveal. Second, keep it a wetland. That's the hitch. Centen-

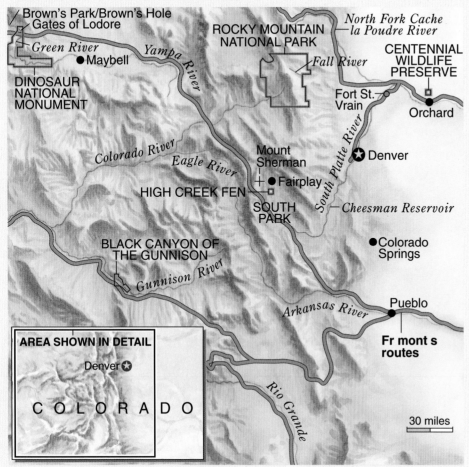

Brown's Park/Brown's Hole
Gates of Lodore
Green River
●Maybell
DINOSAUR NATIONAL MONUMENT
Yampa River
ROCKY MOUNTAIN NATIONAL PARK
North Fork Cache la Poudre River
Fall River
CENTENNIAL WILDLIFE PRESERVE
Fort St. Vrain
Orchard
Colorado River
Eagle River
Mount Sherman
+ ●Fairplay
HIGH CREEK FEN
SOUTH PARK
South Platte River
☆ Denver
─ *Cheesman Reservoir*
BLACK CANYON OF THE GUNNISON
Gunnison River
●Colorado Springs
Arkansas River
Pueblo ●
Fr mont s routes

AREA SHOWN IN DETAIL
Denver ☆
C O L O R A D O
Rio Grande

30 miles

Banks of Biodiversity

Riparian areas—lakeshores and riverbanks and streambanks—have never been extensive in this semi-arid state. Narrow, twisting ribbons of water begin high on mountain slopes as trickles of snowmelt. Then they unroll through valleys and gorges onto the plains. An abundance of plants and animals follows these watercourses. Riparian areas constitute 1 percent of the state's land but support 65 percent of its species. Audrey DeLella Benedict says wetlands throughout the Colorado Rockies "are in jeopardy, doomed to increasing fragmentation."

Riparian banks and shores are a mosaic of trees, shrubs, and grasses, with a species diversity two or three times higher than surrounding landscapes. And unlike the forests, which always wear a dark green uniform, riparian areas change their outfits seasonally. Spring sap ushers in a palette of pale greens and yellows, followed by bright red and purple summer wildflowers and glittering gold leaves in autumn. The plant diversity attracts a variety of animal life, especially birds and small mammals. That's why riparian areas are noisy—often riotous with everything from the croaking of the striped chorus frog to the slapping of beaver tails.

nial controls 1,680 acre feet of water per year—enough to support 2,000 people. Or lots of corn and sugar beets. It's the wet, not the land, that makes the parcel valuable. But Andrick, a former government biologist, opposes draining the site to build a new subdivision or to irrigate farms and suburban lawns. If the new owners exercised water rights to create another 6,000 acres of marsh and ponds, "it would be the largest private wetland in the country," he boasted.

Control and Damage

Frémont followed and forded all the major rivers in Colorado's largest basin, including the main stem of the Colorado River as well as the Green, Yampa, Gunnison, and Eagle rivers. Of those, only the Yampa remains free from a major dam. New dams blocked and diverted water in the Colorado basin through the 1960s, culminating with the Flaming Gorge Dam on the Green River in Wyoming. What were wild, but relatively warm, rivers and floodplains became icy spigots. "The Green runs narrower, deeper, faster and colder," Luecke pointed out. "The dam raises the river's natural spring peak by a factor of five."

Dams killed many native Colorado squawfish, humpback chub, greenback cutthroat trout, and the bonytail chub. Deliberate poisoning nearly eliminated what remained of these native, ancient fish to make room for more sport fish in the river. Attempts to help the natives recover has cost millions of dollars and yielded only mixed results. Young squawfish born in the warmer Yampa often die when they migrate to the Green's colder waters. Some ecologists believe squawfish are better suited to high desert waters, but they were isolated by the Glen Canyon Dam downstream in Utah. Scientists say the humpback chub and the razor-

back are at "reasonable, but lower levels." The bonytail is close to extinction.

The U.S. Fish and Wildlife Service designated 1,980 miles of streams in the Colorado basin as critical for fish survival. It's the largest such designation in the United States and requires agencies to set minimum stream flows. Coloradans don't use all the available river water, and ensuring fish habitat probably wouldn't require much additional volume. But farmers fear the policy will parch their crops, and they are seeking compensation. Said Luecke: "Not everybody agrees on the process, or that it's okay to restore habitat for a self-sustaining native fish population."

Mining's Legacy

Not all of the threats to rivers and their wildlife are modern. A century after its demise, Colorado's mining boom still strangles rivers like the Arkansas. Every day abandoned mines in the Leadville area discharge into the river and its watershed more than 3 million gallons of runoff laden with toxic heavy metals. Zinc, cadmium, lead, arsenic, and copper accumulate in fish, shortening their lives and hampering breeding. In some spots along Chalk Creek and California Gulch, the toxic concentrations are 1,000 times more than what is considered safe for aquatic life.

The poisoning worsens every spring. Snowmelt pulses through heaps of mine tailings, and poisons leach into the watershed. The vigorous runoff churns up sediments, releasing even heavier loads of dissolved

SCULPTED ROCK:

A kayaker studies canyon walls carved by the Green River over eons. This stretch of river, near Brown's Hole, has been tamed by dams built to store water flow and control flooding.

The Fall River shimmers in the morning sun as it snakes through a valley in Rocky Mountain National Park.

There were several beaver dams and several trees recently cut down by beaver. We gave this the name of Beaver Dam Creek, as they are becoming sufficiently rare to distinguish by name the streams on which they are found . . .
It is from this elevated cove and from the gorges of the surrounding mountains, and some lakes within their bosoms, that the great Platte River collects its first waters . . .and certainly no river could ask for a more beautiful origin.

—FRÉMONT
IN SOUTH PARK
JUNE 14, 1845

metals. The pollution, plus government poisonings, wiped out native fish populations decades ago. "Fish can't live normal life spans or reproduce in these waters," said Division of Wildlife aquatic toxicologist Pat Davies. "We rarely find any brown trout over 3 years old."

The state wildlife division has spent $1.25 million to study the impact of heavy metals and other mining pollution on aquatic life in the Arkansas River. The study will have ripple effects statewide. About 1,200 miles of Colorado rivers have suffered from mining pollution; 800 of those miles have been deemed "severely affected," with places that no longer support fish. The Arkansas compounds its own problems because its extremely alkaline, hard water causes metals to bind. The chemical reactions can poison water downstream. In Fort Collins, Davies uses a state-of-the-art maze of tanks, pipes, and automatic diluters to duplicate the river's conditions. The system measures toxins at levels as minute as 100 parts per trillion. Even very low concentrations affect fish mortality, reproduction, and growth.

Denver's Drink

Of the five major river systems that originate in Colorado's mountains, the most commercially important waterway in the state is, ironically, its least impressive. Frémont wouldn't recognize today's South Platte River. Derided by settlers as "a mile wide and an inch deep," now it is dammed and nearly diverted from its headwaters above South Park to the eastern plains. Concrete "streambanks" keep it hustling through Denver, swallowing treated sewage, wrecked cars, and trash. Every drop of water in the river is appropriated to farmers, municipalities, and others with water rights. But that's not enough water to sustain the population along the Front Range.

Snowmelt from the other side of the Continental Divide is diverted through mountain portals to slake metro-area demand. Consequently, South Platte streamflows sometimes run much higher and swifter than Frémont encountered. Or users may reduce the river to a trickle. But the river rarely floods, and thirsty trees and shrubs grow to unnatural densities along its banks. Some water districts want to thin the overgrowth. To assess metro Denver's water needs in the twenty-first century, Governor Roy Romer launched the Front Range Water Forum, a $500,000 study in 1993. Among the panel's proposals in 1998 to reduce water skirmishes among cities, farms, and wildlife advocates is one to allow South Platte water to be used by cities first and then recycled for irrigation. Environmental groups and public agencies are negotiating minimum streamflows to protect high fisheries in Rocky Mountain National Park and on other public lands. A permit to build a dam at Two Forks was denied in 1990 because of the damage its reservoir would have caused to South Platte riverbanks, animal migration routes, and the habitat for a rare butterfly. The federal government's decision more than likely killed dam-building in the West for a generation. "We've moved beyond diverting water and building large storage structures," Luecke said. "Now we're determining how to protect rivers and restore damage."

DARKNESS FALLS:

Sunset casts glorious hues upon the Green River near Brown's Hole in northwestern Colorado. Frémont in 1844 saw a deeper, swifter river that has since been dammed extensively, greatly altering fish, plant, and animal life.

High Creek Fen

Alan Carpenter, land steward for the Nature Conservancy, punches his arm through the boggy soil in the High Creek Fen Preserve in South Park near Fairplay. In this rare plant environment, snowmelt flows not into rivers but into the porous underground, nourishing a huge variety of plants.

SOUTH PARK—Alan Carpenter strode across the undulating meadow as if he were running on a waterbed—all flying elbows and feet. Suddenly he balled up a fist and punched through the grass. The thin air turned musty with a whiff of rotting plants, and his arm disappeared into the underlying muck. "Arrrgghhhh, that's cold," he groaned.

This meadow is a floating mat of vegetation. Underneath is a peat layer that contains 8,000 years of natural history. Not all of Colorado's waters tumble down mountainsides in raging spring torrents. In a few special places, snowmelt constantly gurgles up through the ground. This gentle percolation can nourish a huge variety of plants.

Even in a raw and scabby landscape such as South Park, where glaciers, bison, and peat miners have bulldozed the surface, rare and tiny wildflowers peek from the dense grass. In no place is this soggy miracle better seen than in High Creek Fen, a 1,225-acre wetland preserve that is 9 miles south of Fairplay. Since its discovery in 1991, scientists and amateur botanists have made repeated pilgrimages to this shrine to biodiversity.

Fens, natural niches fed by the mingling of groundwater and rich peat soil, dotted South Park when Frémont passed through 150 years ago. But widespread water diversion projects dried up most of them. Scientifically speaking, High Creek Fen is more than the surviving scrap of a bygone habitat. Biologists declare it is the finest high-elevation peatland in Colorado and probably the southernmost peatland in the United States. It contains thirteen rare plant species, more than any other wetland in the state. The pale blue-eyed grass is rare worldwide. Other plants at the fen are living thousands of miles south of their usual ranges. Three other plant species had never been recorded in Colorado before the High Creek inventory, and three sedge species had been recorded in only a few places. The landlocked wetland also is a haven for shorebirds, including the spotted sandpiper and Wilson's phalarope, as well as a rare snail. "This is a very unusual place," said Carpenter, Colorado land steward for the Nature Conservancy, which purchased the fen from developers. "The plants here are common to Alaska and Greenland, not Colorado."

The nearby mountains established

and mixes with the peat to form a high-octane alkaline fuel for certain fen plants.

The fen is a series of grassy hummocks that resemble footstools. Researchers have found that the plant communities that grow on the tops are very different than those that grow in the wetter troughs between the hummocks. Scientists, who have staked out plots that measure 30 feet by 75 feet, are conducting several long-term experiments to understand how the fen works. Many plots were previously gouged by peat-mining. A state highway crew helped fill in most of the pits with dirt; the rest filled with water. Some of the plots have been reseeded with native plants, while others are being left to restore themselves. Some have peat-rich soil, while a few are barren. The seeded plots are reestablishing rapidly. But even the empty plots are showing promise thanks to wind-blown seeds and seeds that were dormant in the muck. The roles of grazing and wildlife remain to be tested.

The fen is a subtle landscape compared to its majestic surroundings. Most of its important inhabitants measure just a few inches high. Learning how the fen operates could take a lifetime. And that's provided there is no prolonged drought or other extreme change that would complicate the task of reinventing nature here. "I think we're looking at decades, or perhaps a lot longer," Carpenter said. "I'm trying to find out what we should be doing now, so that in thirty years, people will say we had a good idea."

ABUNDANCE:

Rich peat soil mixes with chilly groundwater to create a phenomenal environment for plant life in the High Creek Fen in South Park. Fens once dotted South Park, but extensive water diversion projects to sustain cities and crops dried up most of them.

the fen in this valley that sprawls over an area larger than Rhode Island. South Park sags between the uplifts of several mountain ranges. The valley is an icebox nine months of the year because frigid air sinks to the floor and stays. Plant growth is limited to midsummer. But the cold slows the decomposition of plants, enabling peat layers to accumulate and ultimately enrich the wetlands. Twelve miles west, Mount Sherman, elevation 14,036 feet, and the Mosquito Range supply the water peculiar to the fen. As snowmelt trickles down, it picks up minerals from the mountains' limestone and dolomite formations. The water bubbles up

High Creek Fen's Rare Plants

- **Cottongrass:** Grass ornamental with tufts of white downy material that resembles cotton balls. Found in Colorado's mountain peatlands. Common across Alaska and northern Canada.
- **Greenland primrose:** Common in South Park but uncommon elsewhere in Colorado. Native to Alaska and Canada. Very pale purple-pink flowers measuring a quarter-inch in diameter. Grows in clusters to a height of six inches.
- **Hoary willow:** Found at a few Colorado sites but very common in Alaska. Nicknamed hoary, or frosted, because underside of the green leaf is marked by matted white hairs.
- **Pale blue-eyed grass:** Globally rare plant. Has tiny blue flowers. Cultivated versions have intense blue flowers. Found in small patches in Colorado and Wyoming.
- **Ragwort:** Rare in Colorado. Found in northern latitudes. Orange flower that grows only on top of grassy hummocks in the fen.

COTTONGRASS:

Found in Colorado's mountain peatlands, it is common across Alaska and northern Canada.

The River Otter

It's been several years since Colorado wildlife biologists received their last radio message from a river otter. If this were the space program, NASA would be frantic that its prized satellite hadn't phoned home. But for the Division of Wildlife, silent airwaves don't necessarily trigger alarms. In fact, field researchers are on the verge of declaring that the otters' ranks are self-sustaining, if not increasing. For the biologists, that would mean mission accomplished in the risky business of species reintroduction in the wild. "The otters are pretty much out there on their own now," said non-game wildlife manager Judy Sheppard. "We've had a few reports about seeing young river otters."

Wildlife biologists released 122 otters in the state's river basins between 1976 and 1991, and between 1976 and 1977, the otters established new homes in Cheesman Reservoir, Black Canyon of the Gunnison, the Piedra River, and Rocky Mountain National Park. They came from Oregon, Newfoundland, and Wisconsin in exchange for elk and pine martens. In 1988, another 29 river otters from Oregon were traded for bighorn sheep. Now otters can be found in the upper reaches of the South Platte, the Colorado, the Dolores, and the Cache la Poudre river systems. River otters are elusive, so exact population counts are hard to come by.

Some of the otters were fitted with tiny radio transmitters so biologists could track their movements. But the transmitter batteries eventually died. "Otters do move around a lot, and in some surprising directions and distances," Sheppard said. "I remember one that went straight uphill—away from the river. So it's hard to get a good handle on how many we have."

The river otter, a member of the weasel family, was once among North America's most common mammals. But its dense, oily brown coat became fashionable and by the early 1900s trappers had virtually eliminated it in the West. The otter lives on land but is at home in the water. Belly-flopping down a slick streambank, it tucks its stubby legs beneath its cigar-shaped body and propels itself with powerful tail strokes. Aided by river currents, an adult otter can swim more than a quarter-mile under water. It conserves oxygen under water by slowing its heartbeat. Flaps of skin shut water out of its nostrils and ears. An adult river otter can weigh as much as 30 pounds and measure 4 feet long, tail included. When it's swimming, it can be easily mistaken for a beaver or muskrat. River otter tracks can be mistaken for raccoon tracks. Otters are known for devouring fish, but much of their diet comes from meaty creatures they can catch without expending too much energy, including clams, mussels, snails, reptiles, insects, and birds. The biggest threats to the river otter today are loss of habitat, fish kills, and pollution.

We turned eastward along the upper waters of the stream . . . little valleys with pure crystal water, here leaping swiftly along, and there losing itself in the sand; green spots of luxuriant grass, flowers of all colors . . . To one of these remarkably shaped hills, having on the summit a circular flat rock two or three hundred yards in circumference, someone gave the name Poundcake Rock.

—JOHN C. FRÉMONT
AFTER SEEING PRESENT-DAY CASTLE ROCK,
JULY 9, 1844

River Diary

The Green River grabbed our rubber raft and hurled it downstream.

MAN THE OARS:
Author Joe Verrengia struggles to straighten his raft on the Green River.

BROWN'S PARK—The swift, cold current tugged us toward the quicksand marsh on one side. Then a cold spring wind blew us across the channel against vermilion cliffs. And this is flat water, I reminded myself, as my oars slapped the surface like fly swatters.

John C. Frémont ran the Green River at this spot north of the Gates of Lodore and Dinosaur National Monument 150 years ago. That was long before the Flaming Gorge Dam was built and began regulating streamflow in the upper Green basin in the 1960s. "Frémont would have seen the Green when it was 20 feet deep and twice as fast as it is now," said guide

Patrick Tierney, who doubles as a recreation management professor at San Francisco State University. Tierney gently reclaimed the oars from my deathgrip. He leaned his back into each stroke as the oars knifed into the river. We began to make swift, straight progress.

On the Green River, Frémont used a trapper's skin boat to ferry his cargo downstream. But in 1842, he brought the first inflatable rubber raft to the West, presaging a $70 million seasonal industry in the region. His mission was to survey the Platte River in Wyoming. He loaded the raft with his party's most precious gear, scientific instruments, and collected specimens. Then he added provisions for five men for a dozen days and set off—all without having previously piloted a raft. The Platte's North Fork was running swollen and fierce. Frémont heard the unmistakable roar of rapids through a steep gorge. But the Pathfinder's crew stripped off their clothes and paddled on, loudly singing a now-forgotten tune. "We were, I believe, in the midst of a chorus when the boat struck a concealed rock at the foot of the falls, which whirled her over. . . . Three of my men could not swim. My first feeling was to assist them and save some of our effects. But a sharp concussion or two

FOLLOWING FRÉMONT:

Expedition guide Patrick Tierney readies a raft for a float down the Green River near Brown's Hole where Frémont passed through 150 years ago.

convinced me I had not yet saved myself," the Pathfinder wrote.

Over the next mile and a half, the river claimed virtually all of the party's food, weapons, and gear. Half-naked, the men climbed out of the canyon to rejoin the main party. A barefoot Frémont cut his feet on sharp rocks, but no one drowned. The incident demonstrates that Frémont would rashly risk lives when adventure beckoned. Unbowed, he ordered his men to kill several buffalo for a skin boat. By then, the terrain had leveled and the Platte had returned to its old shallow self. The men pulled the overladen craft for several miles before abandoning it on a sandbar in disgust. Modern-day river guide Tierney has a little Frémont in him. He sports a droopy mustache and a survivalist knife in a shoulder sheath. Before becoming an environmental scientist, Tierney worked as a federal river ranger and commercial guide in the Colorado River basin. Frémont dabbled in botany and species collecting. Tierney has a doctorate in recreation management and ecology from Colorado State University. In the summer, he and his wife, Robin, guide trips for their company, Adrift Adventures of Vernal, Utah. On the river, he implores his rafting customer to stop chattering and appreciate nature's music: the thundering spring runoff, wind rustling the junipers, a cinnamon teal furiously flapping its wings. "The sheer cliffs are what they notice initially," Tierney said. "But soon the biodiversity becomes apparent to them, how the terracing up the slope affects the plant life, from the cottonwoods on the bank to the juniper shrubs at the rim."

PART EIGHT

PROTECTING WHAT'S LEFT

LIVERMORE—RANCHER ED HANSEN LEANED OUT THE PICKUP TRUCK WINDOW AND SURVEYED HIS SPREAD NEAR RED FEATHER LAKES. AFTER FIFTY YEARS OF PUNCHING CATTLE, HE ALLOWED HIMSELF A LITTLE SMILE.

Lush, green pastures of knee-high grass and wild-flowers overrun the surrounding foothills of the laramie mountains. Down the gulch and out of sight, Lone Pine Creek gently gurgles through the meadow toward its confluence with the North Fork of the Cache la Poudre River. Two miles north as the golden eagle flies, the river continues to carve Phantom Canyon from maroon granite bedrock.

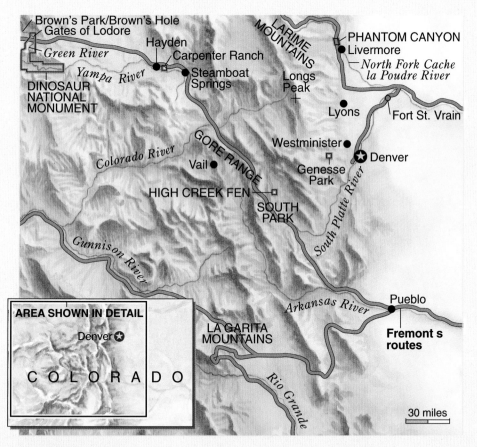

**FRÉMONT'S
ROUTES
THROUGH
COLORADO**

About 150 summers ago, John C. Frémont rode across this range and through the canyon. The

Pathfinder's route remains virtually unchanged from the "very wild and beautiful . . . mountain valley" he described in his journal. A conservation trust protects the canyon. But much of the surrounding landscape remains in the weathered hands of ranchers like Hansen. When he checks his fence lines, he sometimes rides by patches of Ute ladies' tresses orchids and other rare plants. Occasionally he glimpses a bobcat. Nearby, one of the two remaining elk migration routes along the Front Range winds through rugged ravines.

Retaining the Phantom Canyon area's natural assets while earning a living from his cattle has been part of Hansen's approach since he learned to hunt in these hills before World War II. Ceding responsibility to a government scientist or, even worse in his view, a stranger from an environmental group would be an intolerable loss of personal freedom and an insult to what Hansen considers a lifelong record of land stewardship. That's why he opposes the U.S. Biological Service, the nationwide scientific effort to catalog rare species and their habitats. "We're not opposed to change as long as it's done scientifically and fairly," Hansen said. "But if they find something endangered on your land, they can totally shut you down. My herd still has to eat. It's an invasion of private property rights, and it's got people scared. I do not want the U.S. Biological Service on my land."

Biodiversity is Scary

Hansen is not alone. Many people in Colorado who earn their living off the land—ranchers, farmers, loggers, even some recreation outfitters—are convinced

Where a farmer sees a cash crop at the end of his sprinkler"s rainbow, naturalists lament the plowing under of the shortgrass prairie. As the explorer Frémont approached Long's Peak (visible at right) from the eastern plains 150 years ago, he crossed a dense mat of grasses bursting with sunflowers. Those flowers still straggle upward, but on this modern farm they're just weeds.

that environmental regulations are geared to punish them. The fact that the U.S. Biological Service must receive written permission to survey on private land and is required to disclose its survey findings provides no reassurance. "These landowners are afraid of biodiversity issues," said William Riebsame. "They're afraid somebody will find a Black-footed ferret on their property or say they found evidence of one."

The chasm between ranchers and environmentalists is wide and deep. Among the champions of private property rights is Senator Wayne Allard (R-Colorado). During his career in Congress, Allard has unsuccessfully tried to eliminate the biological service's $170 million annual operating budget as part of broader effort to champion western property rights. The U.S. Biological Service "empowers bureaucrats and environmental

A cow peers under a Nature Conservancy sign marking the High Creek Fen, a recently discovered peatland 9 miles south of Fairplay in South Park. The Nature Conservancy purchased the 1,067-acre wetland and is preserving it.

crusaders," Allard said. "I believe that it marks another milestone on the road to diminished private property rights."

On the other side of the fence, the National Wildlife Federation and others accuse ranchers of allowing livestock to "graze to extinction" hundreds of species living on private and public lands in the West, including no fewer than nine plant and animal species in Colorado. But a growing number of ecologists say they are saddened by the increasing rancor and suspicion that blacken the conservation debate. As they survey biodiversity throughout the state every summer, they find places where the impact of grazing and other commercial activities is being reduced. Many say they recognize that ranching is integral to the rural economy and won't be dislodged. They hope that the same ranchers, loggers, and others stop "overreacting" and learn to share their appreciation for Colorado's thousands of species and their desire to protect them. "Ranchers have gotten the wrong message, and it's so sad," said Boris Kondratieff, an entomologist at Colorado State University. "Nobody is out to get them or take their land. I don't know of a single case where a rancher lost land because of biodiversity."

Species Act Endangered?

The biological survey debate is a dress rehearsal for the disagreement over the Endangered Species Act. It's the nation's toughest —and most controversial—conservation law. The act requires congressional reauthorization, which has been delayed by successive congresses.

Supporters credit the act with keeping several rare species and their habitats from oblivion. The bald eagle is cited frequently. There were only 400 breeding pairs in the lower 48 states in 1973. By 1998 there were more than 5,000 pairs; the bald eagle was redesignated from an endangered specier to a threatened species.

Biologists believe as many as 9,000 species of plants and animals in the United States are threatened or endangered. They blame commercial and residential development, draining of the wetlands, and the building of new roads. Fewer than 20 percent of these rare species are directly protected under federal law. A major test case in the offing is the black-tailed prairie dog. The Biodiversity Legal Foundation wants federal agencies to declare thousands of eastern plains acres as critical habitat for the prairie dog and the dozens of species, including birds of prey, that hunt it for food and use its burrows. Foundation officials want to see the Endangered Species Act strengthened and streamlined so more habitat and species can be protected. "If it was left up to local interests, we wouldn't have any species left," said Jasper Carlton. "You don't get anywhere with species conservation if you don't go to court."

Opponents hope to increase the rights of property owners and economic considerations in species-recovery plans as part of any new Endangered Species Act. They point to the northern spotted owl as proof the law has run amok. Since 1989, federal court injunctions have put nearly 5 million acres of Pacific Northwest timberland off-limits for fear of wiping out the owl's habitat. Timber-related jobs dropped by 50 percent, a consequence, opponents say, of conservation efforts more than a downturn in the timber market. "We have weight-

Buffer Zones

In addition to incentives, environmentalists suggest several approaches that would significantly change activities on public and private lands close to important habitats. Ranchers and other landowners, however, resist many of the changes because they would mean additional regulations or declaring productive land and other resources off-limits. Establishing buffer zones where development is restricted is the conservationists' biggest priority. Otherwise, they say, every park and natural monument risks tourist development like that on the boundary of Rocky Mountain National Park. Inside the park's borders is an elk's world. But a few feet away is Estes Park, a vacationer's paradise of rock shops and giant water slides. The Foundation of Deep Ecology, which awards grants to biodiversity projects, has suggested surrounding "core areas"—national parks, wilderness areas, and national monuments—with layers of buffer zones. Human use would be more strictly regulated within these zones as they creep closer to park boundaries.

Conservation biologist Rick Knight suggests a compromise: the designation of working ranches as buffer zones, with ranchers and environmentalists jointly managing programs for rare species in the areas. Knight's suggestion serves two purposes: protecting biodiversity and preserving the historic ranching lifestyle. One practice Knight would like to curtail is the subdivision of ranches across Colorado into 40-acre "ranchettes" for retirement and vacation homes. The plots are too small to support livestock, but they chop up open spaces that wildlife requires. Knight recom-

IRRIGATION MOSAIC: *"The soil of all this country is excellent . . . and would support a large agricultural and pastoral population." Frémont's observations proved prophetic, as is vividly demonstrated by this march of crop circles across the San Luis Valley. The deeper green circular patterns are crops watered by center-pivot irrigation systems.*

ed everything in terms of these animals, and then given no consideration to economics or to communities," said Barbara Grinnell, executive director of People for the West, a Pueblo-based group that promotes the commercial use of natural resources. "Mainstream America is asking what we are doing with these species. It defies common sense."

There is some common ground. People on both sides want to give landholders incentives for protecting rare species. A possible motivation would be money. Landowners could be paid to protect endangered species and their habitats. Tacking on conservation and biodiversity fees to park admissions and establishing backcountry fees for camping, bird-watching, and other activities could provide some of the funding. "We have enough clubs in the Endangered Species Act, but not enough honey," Carlton said. "Ranchers want independence, but they like to be seen as good conservationists," he pointed out. "We need to add positive reinforcements."

BUFFALO RANCHING:
Rancher Paul Jonjak checks on the buffalo he is raising northwest of Lyons. Described by Frémont as too numerous to count, buffalo were nearly extinct at the turn of the century. Raising them as an increasingly popular source of meat has helped bring the buffalo back, even if they no longer range freely.

mends communities pass ordinances requiring that new homes be built in clusters, which would leave most of the land for wildlife and recreation.

Linking Parks

"What we're doing now," said David Armstrong, "is breaking an extremely narrow peninsula of biodiversity into islands." Most of those islands are public preserves. Some, like national forests, are sprawling. But many, like Roxborough State Park and the Denver mountain parks, are scattered spaces surrounded by neighborhoods and roads. Even some parks are fragmented. Genesee Park in Jefferson County is split by Interstate 70. "Suppose you have a female black bear on one side of the park and a male bear on the other side," said Laurie Roulston, a science educator at the Denver Museum of Natural History. "Either that male risks crossing the highway or they're not going to breed."

Researchers and officials of some foothills communities are discussing ways to build biodiversity bridges between these islands in the form of trails and land acquisitions. One plan debated in Jefferson County would create a "linear park system" by connecting existing public lands. The linear park would run north to south and would include land in Larimer, Boulder, Jefferson, Douglas, and El Paso counties. But even such a well-intentioned plan has drawbacks. Scientists aren't sure if a linear park would simulate wildlife migration corridors, or if it would cause new problems. "We know very little about wildlife corridors" admitted Chris Pague. "And corridors introduce other species, such as weeds and rats. They would have to be intensively managed to a degree we have not anticipated."

Knowledge is Power

Conservationists realize they cannot stop all new construction, but wonder if construction can offer a new opportunity. Those who undertake new construction are already required to submit to electrical, plumbing, and fire safety inspections. Some biologists would like to add a fourth permit—biodiversity. Before construction they suggest, builders and landowners should know what lives on the property. If they find a rare plant, for example, construction would have to be oriented so it did not disturb that plant. "The question," said Judy Sheppard, "is who would pay for it."

The Colorado Natural Heritage Program already conducts biodiversity surveys on public and private lands. Agencies and developers call the program 1,000 times a year seeking information on Colorado sites. Private landowners can call, too, free of charge. "We need to empower landowners with information," agreed Pague. "Private owners don't knowingly harm their property."

Conversation with a Naturalist

Automobile taillights and headlights on the Boulder Turnpike add their own hues to the sunset in this time-exposure photograph. Where Frémont followed rivers as natural pathways into the Front Range foothills and the Rocky Mountains beyond, today's travelers follow the highways.

Edward O. Wilson is the champion of biodiversity. In the 1980s, the Harvard University professor alerted the world that humankind was rapidly depleting nature without knowing what it contained. The wholesale destruction of tropical rain forests, coral reefs, and other habitats, he and others warned, would inevitably be followed by a tide of species extinctions that could not be reversed. Wilson has won two Pulitzer Prizes and a slew of scientific awards. He has written an intensely personal and revealing memoir, *Naturalist.*

JV: You said that humanity was facing the ultimate catastrophe in widespread species extinctions because its effects couldn't be reversed in a few generations. Looking back, would you change your forecast?

Wilson: In one sense, it is worse now. The destruction has accelerated since then. The reduction of the tropical rain forest has accelerated. But there is improvement in that the science of conservation biology has advanced greatly. We know much more about the details of extinction. Public opinion has changed somewhat, too, toward conservation. In the 1980s, it was an almost invisible issue.

JV:: Biodiversity is a political term now. It became mainstream during the environmental summit in Rio de Janeiro in 1992, when the United States refused to sign a treaty establishing biodiversity as part of a nation's heritage and property.

Wilson: I think, in an unintended way, President [George] Bush brought biodiversity onto center stage by refusing to sign the international biodiversity treaty. In the long term, he probably did us more good.

JV: As a child, you found refuge in the ponds and woods of Alabama. Do children today manage to find similar refuge in nature where they live?

Wilson: I was innately attracted to wilderness from the beginning. It was fascinating to discover new creatures at every turn of the path or every yard of a beach walk. It was an enormous stimulus. I think there were two great stimuli in my childhood: nature and fairy tales. They overlapped. More and more, children are enclosed in an almost unbreakable cocoon of urban and suburban dwellings. The percentage of children that has easy access to nature has been declining steadily in this century. The positive aspect is that a child does not need an ocean or mountain range to enjoy the full range of wonders of nature. A weedy, vacant lot or a city park can be enough.

JV: How is nature important to a child?

Wilson: Two aspects of nature ought to be stressed in its effect on a child's developing mind. The first is that nature is vastly more complex than the world of artifacts. There always is more to discover. And the second important thing is that children are innately attracted to nature. They find it easy and natural to identify with plants and animals in wild environments. And I believe those two qualities are why animals and plants and wild lands continue to play such a prominent role in our culture.

JV: The University of Alabama gave you lab space when you were 17 to pursue a career in entomology. Bug studies don't bring in big research dollars. Would a university make room for that young man today?

Wilson: I think it would happen in some universities. It's important for young people to recognize that to do science one doesn't have to don a white coat and learn to work partial differential equations or go into abstract theory and high technology. There is a royal road into science that comes from fieldwork, entering through ecology and conservation biology. Environmental studies have a whole relevance to new professions. I wish I could do it all over again. If you study the lives of scientists, even those who end up in math or physics or molecular biology were fascinated by some intricate puzzle or beautiful pattern they experienced when very young. Mine was with nature. It's the art of the human condition to experience that kind of revelation at an early age. That should be considered as a potentially very potent first step toward becoming a scientist. You don't have to have the upper reaches of the Amazon as a pristine wilderness. If you bring your scale down to the microscopic, wilderness can be in a handful of soil just outside the door.

JV: You're an activist now. But in your memoir you recall that you were troubled for years by not speaking out. What was preventing you?

Wilson: The number of people capable of, and willing to be, honest brokers in providing scientific information was quite small. Ecology and biodiversity were very unfashionable in the 1960s and 1970s. There are relatively few of us now who are reluctant to speak out. Politics now doesn't frighten many scientists. A lot of them are cautious, and they should be. But it is no longer taboo, especially in environmental matters.

JV: When it was coined, you resented the term biodiversity.

Wilson: I wanted to call it biological diversity. I thought it would sound more dignified. Biodiversity sounded a little too catchy to me, like a word invented by advertising, and I thought it wouldn't be taken seriously. Luckily, I was persuaded otherwise.

JV: At the end of your memoir you declare, "Earth, in its dazzling variety of life, is still a little known planet . . . and I will be an explorer naturalist until I die."

Wilson: In the end, that's what I got from writing the book. I am proud to identify myself as a naturalist.

STRANDED:

Highways and housing development create islands of biodiversity in metro Denver.

The Yampa

Most rivers in Colorado rush like a cavalry charge toward the sea.

REFLECTIONS:

Cottonwood reflections shimmer in a pool of the Yampa River near the Carpenter Ranch.

Dams make them behave that way. But the Yampa slithers slowly, like a snake. It has just one dam straddling its banks in the foothills of the Gore Range. The Yampa is an oddity in the Colorado River basin, where other major rivers are straitjacketed by dams and dikes. Some of the dams are made from whatever's handy—including junked cars.

The Nature Conservancy has declared one of this river's many kinks a globally rare plant community worth saving, because its banks are lined with cottonwood, box elder, and red-osier dogwood. The group already owns 5 miles of river frontage on the adjacent Carpenter Ranch. "This type of riverbank forest probably never was widespread because there aren't very many wide valleys at such a high elevation," explained Colorado State University ecologist Holly Richter, who now works for the Conservancy in Arizona. She simulated the Yampa's serpentine ways on a computer. "But these habitats have declined because reservoir construction and water diversions have changed the rivers' hydrology, too," she said.

The challenge for conservationists is how to keep the Yampa the Yampa and how to prevent it from becoming a clone of its dammed and diverted cousin, the Green River. Conservation easements are rapidly becoming a popular option. There are more than 200 land trusts in Colorado. The easements, which are often quicker to accomplish than purchases by a federal agency, reduce taxes for the landowners' families and protect open space from development. Easements are particularly important near ski resorts like Steamboat Springs, which is 19 miles east of the Carpenter Ranch. With a pair of preserves protected, the Nature Conservancy hopes to study the river's seasonal flood-and-drain cycle and protect the flourishing biodiversity in a rapidly developing area.

The river has changed little since John C. Frémont remarked on the Yampa Valley's lush grass and thick cottonwoods in 1844. Farrington Carpenter established his family's ranch here a century ago. Since then the river has added even more curves and kinks. Its wetlands attract the common yellowthroat warbler and other disappearing songbird species. Along its main channel, a cottonwood forest offers roosts for bald eagles and browsing for elk. The Nature Conservancy is returning cattle to the ranch as well. With the support of the Carpenter family, it intends to demonstrate ways in which ranching and nature can prosper side by side. The emerging lessons could help solve overgrazing and the trampling of streambeds in the West. "We want to conserve the river in a way that is compatible with the people who depend on it to make their livings," said Conservancy spokesman Jamie Williams. "We know a lot about the river's biological significance. But they know how a ranch depends on the river," he said. "When it's 40 below in the winter, the cottonwoods provide important shelter for cattle."

Using ground surveys and six decades of aerial photos, Richter mapped the floodplain at the Carpenter Ranch and is cataloging its lush biodiversity for the Conservancy. She is especially interested in an abandoned river channel near the ranch buildings. When a river abandons its historic channel and carves a new one, the old channel turns into an oxbow lake. It sags and becomes a cattail marsh. Eventually, willow shrubs fill in the saturated soil. During spring, the swollen main channel chews soil from the outside bank and dumps it on the inner bank. These new gravel bars become nurseries for cottonwood and box elder seedlings. Richter's model can predict how the Yampa and the Carpenter Ranch habitat would fare if, say, another dam were added or if water use doubled. Grazing is her bigger concern. It will take years of close scrutiny to determine whether the cattle are decimating some plant species, driving away wildlife, and compacting the saturated soils. The Conservancy maintains fences along parts of the riverbank, and it is offering to help neighbors do the same. But the ranch's new environmental partner is convinced that grazing and conservation can coexist. "We don't know what the impact of grazing will be on this habitat," Richter said. "But we can learn it scientifically."

YAMPA VALLEY:

The thick cottonwoods and lush grass that Frémont described in the Yampa Valley in 1844 remain little changed today on the Carpenter Ranch, 19 miles west of Steamboat Springs. With the support of the Carpenter family, the Nature Conservancy plans to use this area to demonstrate ways that ranching and nature can coexist.

ON A ROCKY SLOPE NEAR THE GREEN RIVER:

Golden aster grows in dry, sunny areas and can flourish in deserts and fields as well as on hillsides and rocky slopes. Asters make an excellent choice for a low-water garden addition.

Low-Water Plants

Once these plants are established, little, if any, additional irrigation is required.

TREES
Burr oak
Piñon pine

SHRUBS
Curleaf mountain
  mahogany
New Mexican privet
Mexican cliffrose
Sand cherry
Shrubby sage
Three-leaf sumac

GROUND COVERS
Creeping juniper
Creeping red
  penstemon
Fringed sage
Hardy ice plant
Pussytoes
Snow-in-summer
Sulfur flower
Wooly thyme

PERENNIALS
Blanket flower
Blue flax
Gayfeather
Golden aster
Prairie coneflower
Rocky Mountain
  penstemon
Silverleaf cinquefoil

ANNUALS
Annual baby's breath
Annual coreopsis
California poppy
Mountain bachelor
  button
Statice

SOURCE:
AURORA UTILITIES
DEPARTMENT

The Bluegrass Blues

Coloradans are partial to cowboy hats and sport utility vehicles. So when they buy their houses, why do they turn into eccentric English gardeners? Every spring, homeowners unroll sod carpets of lush, thirsty bluegrass and plant dozens of annual flower varieties in the dense clay soil of the Front Range. Metro Denver receives an average of only 14 inches of rain a year. More than half the water used by a typical family gets dumped on the lawn, and landscapers estimate that 85 percent of a yard's health problems stem from overwatering. Botanists and extension agents discourage the planting of nonnative flowers, but New Guinea impatiens and tulips are big business. Many subdivisions have covenants requiring landscaping to conform to a standard suburban appearance without accounting for local conditions and climate.

Then there are the foothills communities. Higher elevations and cooler nights turn the pseudo-English gardening strategy into pure folly. But people persist because, they explain, it makes a house look like a home. "There are many landscaped yards in the Denver-Boulder area that have a higher biodiversity than Rocky Mountain National Park," said Yan Linhart. "But most of these species in people's yards are exotics— alien species that have been introduced," he said. "We are very successful at it, because we use fertilizers, pesticides, and diverted water."

Native and dryland plants can be beautiful, and because they typically use less water, they can be easier to maintain. They also attract more birds and other wildlife. Frémont described them in his journals: lupens, clematis, delphiniums of "green and a lustrous metallic blue," prairie coneflower, and, most of all, blue flax. Landscaping with native plants requires a little planning. Don't do everything in a week or even one summer. Follow these rules before you dig up your yard:

1. Learn what grows in your area. Visit a nearby outdoor education center. Take a seminar in native plants or xeriscaping (which translates into dryland gardening). Or visit a foothills park and bring a field guide to identify what's growing wild. Then take a list of your favorites to a nursery and buy their commercially bred cousins.

2. Before you plant, improve your soil with aged manure and other organic material. After you plant, spread wood chips and other mulch around plants to conserve water and keep them cooler.

3. Limit the amount of grass in your yard with ground cover, wooden decking, or a patio. Consider grass varieties other than bluegrass. Researchers are developing residential varieties of buffalo grass, a tough prairie shortgrass that Frémont repeatedly identified. It's very resistant to drought and compaction, but its "green" season is comparatively short. Buffalo grass seed typically requires two growing seasons to establish.

IMPOSING SUMMIT:
"This morning we caught the first faint glimpse of the Rocky Mountains, about 60 miles distant . . . and we were just able to discern the snowy summit of Longs Peak," Frémont wrote July 9, 1842, on his first expedition. A vantage point in Rocky Mountain National Park provides a much closer view.

DIARY OF ENCHANTMENT

GATES OF LODORE—ON THE BANKS OF THE GREEN RIVER, I FOUND A BLUE HONEYBEE TREMBLING ON THE PETALS OF A HOT PINK WILDFLOWER. NOW THAT'S BIODIVERSITY. YOU MAY THINK COLORADO HAS BEEN COMPLETELY EXPLORED IN THE PAST 150 YEARS FROM THE EASTERN GRASSLANDS TO THE ALPINE TUNDRA ATOP THE CONTINENTAL DIVIDE TO THE STIFLING HOT WESTERN CANYONS THAT MARK THE BOUNDARY OF THE FORBIDDING COLORADO PLATEAU. PEOPLE WHO SPEND ALL WEEK SITTING IN CLIMATE-CONTROLLED OFFICES CHARGE INTO THE OUTDOORS ON THE WEEKENDS IN SEARCH OF ADVENTURE AND IN THE PROCESS TRAVERSE FAR MORE TERRITORY THAN EXPLORERS LIKE JOHN C. FRÉMONT COULD ONLY DREAM OF COVERING. THEY'VE BAGGED ALL FIFTY-FOUR OF COLORADO'S 14,000-FOOT PEAKS, FISHED EVERY GOLD MEDAL TROUT STREAM, HIKED THE 470 MILES OF THE COLORADO TRAIL, KAYAKED EVERY HAIR-RAISING STRETCH OF CLASS V WHITE-WATER, AND SKIED THE BACKCOUNTRY COMMANDO RUN BEHIND VAIL. THEY CLAIM TO KNOW COLORADO.

And they do—at least its high-octane extremes, where every trip outdoors turns into an epic struggle against nature. Thrill-seeking was part of Frémont's being, just as it is among rock climbers today. He dared to blindly lead an expedition across the La Garita

A blue honeybee finds nectar on a blooming shrub along the Green River near Brown's Hole.

Mountains in midwinter largely because everyone told him not to risk it. It was the 1848 version of free solo-climbing up the cliffs of Eldorado Canyon. If Frémont was alive today, he would likely trade his sodden buckskins for a Gore-Tex suit and his old India rubber raft for a custom-molded kayak made of carbon-injected fibers.

But what's often lost in the mythology surrounding the Pathfinder is his introspective side. Frémont was a passionate naturalist who appreciated the small and the obscure. Which brings me back to the blue honeybee. I found it by accident while rafting the Green. We had put into shore for a pit stop; emerging from the piñon pine and juniper underbrush, I wandered down the rocky ledge to get a closer look at the cliffs we had been hurtling past. First I saw the flowers—they were the only splash of color in a brown arid landscape. Then I saw the bee's metallic blue body vibrating and glinting in the sun as it collected nectar and pollen. Our encounter lasted for a moment. I leaned so close that I almost brushed my nose against its bristly back. Then it buzzed off to continue doing the bee thing in the brief time when the wildflowers bloom.

But why blue? Dinosaur National Monument has an estimated 3,000 insect species and fewer than 100 sport iridescent colors. Entomologist Boris Kondratieff said the unusual blue color is the result of light scattering through the layers and imperfections of the bee's external skeleton. At some angles, reflecting light would make the bee appear green rather than blue. These "metallic" insects are more common in the tropics. Kondratieff said the bright blue color could be a breeding cue, a strategy to warn predators, or even an advertisement that the bee has a dangerous sting. The blue bee symbolizes another kind of Colorado adventure, more of an enchantment than a self-induced heart attack on a mogul ski run.

The state is full of them. You can crawl across 100 feet of alpine tundra and see a half-dozen plant communities with different butterflies on each. Or watch a great blue heron lumber into the air like a B-52 from the South Platte River. Or stare into a bison's eyes and feel as if you had stepped into the pages of Frémont's own journals. A bee taught Frémont a biodiversity lesson, too. It was during his first expedition; it wasn't in Colorado, but on Gannett Peak in Wyoming's Wind River Range. He had just unfurled the American flag on the summit where, he recalled,

ISLAND OF NATURE:
Blacktop and Westminster houses bound a small patch of natural prairie that was willed to the Nature Conservancy at Wadsworth Parkway and West 108th Avenue.

The stillness was absolute, unbroken by any sound, and the solitude complete. We thought ourselves beyond the region of any animated life. A solitary bee came winging his flight from the eastern valley, and lit on the knee of one of the men. It was a strange place, the icy rock and the highest peak, for a lover of warm sunshine and flowers; and we pleased ourselves with the idea that he was the first of his species to cross the mountain barrier—a solitary pioneer to foretell the advance of civilization.

Here is where Frémont and I part company. It never occurred to me on the banks of the Green River that I might take my blue bee home, like a pebble from the riverbank or a commemorative sun visor from the Dinosaur National Monument gift shop. But Frémont was a man of his times. He flattened his bee in a book. "I believe that a moment's thought would have made us let him continue his way unharmed," the Pathfinder wrote.

But we carried out the law of this country, where all animated nature seems to be at war; and seizing him immediately put him in at least a fit place— in the leaves of a large book among the flowers we had collected along the way.

Glossary

Alpine: Treeless region on mountaintops and high ridges.

Biodiversity: The assembly of life in a given area at a level strong enough to perpetuate itself despite occasional setbacks.

Conifer: Tree or shrub with needle leaves. Often evergreen that bears its seeds in cones.

Deciduous: A plant that sheds its leaves in fall.

Ecological zone: The geographical area defined by a large ecosystem, such as the foothills.

Ecosystem: All the living organisms, plus the physical factors that affect them, working as a single unit in a particular place and time.

Endangered species: A plant or animal designated by the federal government as rarely found in nature and in grave danger of extinction. The designation is based upon population, remaining habitat, or both.

Eradication: A government-funded effort to kill an organism that damages crops, preys on livestock or causes economic losses.

Exotic species: Non-native plants introduced to a region. Some are deliberately planted, but most arrive accidentally. Also known as weeds.

Fen: Wetland in which plants are fed by both groundwater and surface runoff. Nutrients from peat deposits produce a rich variety of plants.

Foothills: Low mountain ranges between 5,500 and 8,000 feet. Site of intense development between Fort Collins and Colorado Springs.

Forest: A large tract of land covered with trees and undergrowth.

Fragmentation: The breakup of the habitat of a plant or animal. Usually caused by development, road-building, or other human activities.

Grammanoids: Various native grasses common on the tundra and prairie.

Grassland: A dry, rolling treeless landscape below elevation 5,600 feet. Other names include shortgrass prairie, tallgrass prairie, and plains.

Minimum stream flow: The lowest water level required to support fish, insects, and other wildlife.

Native species: Plants that existed in a region before white exploration and settlement in the nineteenth century.

Old-growth: A mature, healthy forest with many trees at their extreme range of age and size. Each species has its own old-growth threshold. Piñon-juniper old-growth is 100 years; for some conifers, it is more than 300 years.

Remnant prairie: Small, random parcels of the original grasslands containing mostly native species.

Riparian ecosystem: A narrow, moist zone along the banks of a river or the shore of a lake. Often supports plants and animals that are different from those in the surrounding countryside.

Saxicoline: Plants inhabiting dry, rocky places.

Semiarid: A landscape characterized by light rainfall and capable of supporting only shortgrasses and shrubs.

Semidesert: An arid or semiarid transitional region located between the desert and either grassland or woodland. Contains sparse, shrubby vegetation.

Talus: Sloping mass of rocky fragments below a cliff.

Transition zone: Area where species from two or more ecological zones overlap.

Tundra: A treeless ecosystem above timberline in the mountains or lying very far north.

Watershed: The area below a ridge line that drains into a river.

Suggested Reading

PART ONE

Frémont, John C., *Report of the Expeditions to the Rocky Mountains.* Washington, D.C.: Smithsonian Institution Press, 1988.

Nevins, Allan, Frémont: *Pathmarker of the West.* Lincoln: University of Nebraska Press, 1992

Rolle, Andrew, John Charles Frémont: *Character as Destiny.* Norman: University of Oklahoma Press, 1991.

PART TWO

Benedict, Audrey DeLella, *A Sierra Club Naturalist's Guide: The Southern Rockies.* San Francisco: Sierra Club Books, 1991.

Mutel, Cornelia Fleischer and Emerick, John C., *From Grassland to Glacier.* Boulder, Colo.: Johnson Books, 1984.

PART THREE

Armstrong, David M., *Rocky Mountain Mammals.* Niwot: University of Colorado Press, 1989.

Dary, David A., *The Buffalo Book: The Full Story of the American Animal.* Chicago: Sage, 1974.

Evans, Howard Ensign, *Pioneer Naturalists: The Discovery and Naming of North American Plants and Animals.* New York: Henry Holt Publishing, 1993.

PART FOUR

Carter, Jack, *Trees and Shrubs of Colorado.* Boulder, Colo.: Johnson Books, 1988.

Zwinger, Ann, *Beyond the Aspen Grove.* New York: Random House, 1970.

PART FIVE

Helmuth, Ed, and Helmuth, Gloria, *The Passes of Colorado: An Encyclopedia of Watershed Divides.* Boulder, Colo.: Pruett Publishers, 1994.

Tilden, J.W., and Smith, Arthur C., *Peterson Field Guide to Western Butterflies.* Boston: Houghton Mifflin, 1986.

Smith, Dwight, *Above Timberline.* Boulder, Colo.: Pruett Publishers, 1980.

PART SIX

Leydet, Francois, *The Coyote.: Defiant Songdog of the West.* Norman: University of Oklahoma Press, 1988.

Weber, William A., *Rocky Mountain Flora: Western Slope.* Rev. ed. Niwot, Colo.: University of Colorado Press, 1996.

Zindahl, Robert M., *Weeds of Colorado.* Fort Collins, Colo.: Colorado State University Extension, Bulletin 521A.

PART SEVEN

Evans, Howard Ensign, and Evans, Mary Alice, *Cache la Poudre: The Natural History of a Rocky Mountain River.* Niwot, Colo.: University of Colorado Press, 1993.

Ward, J.C., and Kondratieff, Boris C., *Illustrated Guide to the Mountain Stream Insects of Colorado.* Niwot, Colo.: University of Colorado Press, 1992.

Zwinger, Ann, *Run, River, Run: A Naturalist's Journey Down the Green River.* Tucson: University of Arizona Press, 1975, 4th 1996.

PART EIGHT

Wilson, E.O., *Naturalist.* Washington D.C.: Island Press, 1994

Index